http:// united st

WORKPLACE
LEARNING
PRINCIPLES AND PRACTICE

The Professional Practices in Adult Education and Lifelong Learning Series explores issues and concerns of practitioners who work in the broad range of settings in adult and continuing education and lifelong learning

The books provide information and strategies on how to make practice more effective for professionals and those they serve. They are written from a practical viewpoint and provide a forum for instructors, administrators, policy makers, counselors, trainers, instructional; designers, and other related professionals. the series contains single author or coauthored books only and does not include edited volumes.

Sharan B. Merriam
Ronald M. Cervero
Series Editors

WORKPLACE
LEARNING
PRINCIPLES AND PRACTICE

Robert W. Rowden

KRIEGER PUBLISHING COMPANY
MALABAR, FLORIDA
2007

Original Edition 2007

Printed and Published by
KRIEGER PUBLISHING COMPANY
KRIEGER DRIVE
MALABAR, FL 32950

Library of Congress Cataloging-in-Publication Data

Rowden, Robert W. (Robert Wayne), 1947-
    Workplace learning : principles and practice / Robert W. Rowden.
      p. cm. — (The professional practices in adult education and lifelong learning series)
    Includes bibliographical references and index.
    ISBN 1-57524-268-0 (alk. paper)
    1. Organizational learning. 2. Employees—Training of. 3. Career development. 4. Adult learning. I. Title. II. Series.

HD58.82.R69 2007
658.3'124—dc22
                                    2006046472

10 9 8 7 6 5 4 3 2

This book is dedicated to Sharan, my wife.
Without her love, support, and encouragement
it never would have happened.

CONTENTS

Preface   ix

The Author   xiii

1.   Exploring the Concept   1

2.   Environmental Factors   19

3.   Individual Learning   39

4.   Social and Group Dimensions of
       Workplace Learning   57

5.   Organizational Learning   77

6.   Moving from Training to Workplace Learning   97

7.   The Future of Workplace Learning   113

References   131

Index   143

PREFACE

Over the past 75 years or so there has been considerable emphasis placed on the importance of work-related training and development, and more recently this interest has been extended to the concept of workplace learning. Many organizations have had to consider the role of learning in their workforce in light of the rapid change in the world, competition between local and international organizations, and the need to improve worker skills. Organizations are also focusing on ways they can be assisted in meeting the new demands being placed upon them by this ever-changing environment. Still, even while organizations recognize the need to improve workers' skills, the concept of workplace learning and how to facilitate it is surrounded by confusion and indecision. Workplace learning is an extremely complex concept that goes way beyond the traditional model of training. [Workplace learning] is an emerging interdisciplinary field that encompasses the theory and practice of management and leadership, individual and organizational learning, formal, informal and incidental learning, and training, development and education, that takes place within the workplace. An understanding of workplace learning requires the integration of a range of concepts such as adult learning, career development, organizational learning, and individual interests. The nature of the work climate, the use of technology, the teaching and learning styles used, the perception of learning in and for the workplace have an impact on how learning takes place—or not.

I became interested in the various ways that workers learn to do their jobs more than 15 years ago. At that time, I was conducting a study of the role that Human Resource Development (HRD) played in the success of small businesses in the United States. I selected a number of small businesses that had been successful for several years. I began the qualitative inquiry by interviewing the owner or president. Understandably, the first question I asked was, "Tell me about the types and kind of HRD you do in your company." The response was not what I expected to hear. To a person, they all said something like, "Well, we really don't do any. I really believe in it but we just don't have the time or the money."

Being undaunted by this—or maybe just too naive to know better—I pressed on. Good thing I did. After interviewing the owners, managers, and workers at all levels, I found that, in fact, they did do a lot of "HRD" in their organizations—they just didn't call it that. Their model of understanding was based on what they had come to know as HRD in larger businesses—TRAINING. To them, if employees weren't sitting in a classroom they weren't learning. But by probing deeper, it was revealed that in addition to the formal learning that was available, a lot of informal learning and incidental learning was a part of their everyday life. This realization of what goes on in organizations led to the development of a survey instrument to measure workplace learning that has been used successfully in more than seven additional studies. These research findings have helped solidify the presence of workplace learning in organizations. The findings have also emphasized the need to build awareness of workplace learning so that the next time someone asks workers about their workplace learning they won't say—"Well, we really don't do any." Maybe the information in this book will help.

Chapter 1 provides a brief overview of the concept of workplace learning. Discussed are some of the key premises that draw heavily on adult learning theory. The idea of learning as part of everyday thinking and acting in the workplace is illustrated. There is a discussion of learning as a *process* rather than a *product*. The key concepts of training, human resource development, and workplace learning are compared.

Chapter 2 explores the *internal* and *external* factors that influence workplace learning. Factors such as the organization's climate and culture and leadership all influence learning opportunities within the organization. External factors such as "globalization," outsourcing of jobs to other countries, downsizing/rightsizing/reorganizing, and competition and changing markets impact workplace learning. Of great importance is the development of a climate conducive to workplace learning.

Chapter 3 continues the exploration of workplace learning by looking at the processes involved in learning at the individual level. The chapter draws heavily on adult learning theory and looks at cognitive processes in workplace learning. A holistic learning *process* is appropriate for today's fast-paced organizations, rather than a *product* exemplified by training. Self-directed learning and informal learning are explored as well as ways to facilitate individual learning in the workplace.

Chapter 4 discusses how learning is a social endeavor and how people use learning to construct meaning of the context they encounter. Informal groups are formed by workers engaged in shared activities who wish to learn what other members know. Social interaction in work teams promotes learning and identity, develops communities of practice, and fosters workplace learning.

Chapter 5 explores workplace learning from an organizational level. The role of workplace learning in different organizational concepts such as the Learning Organization, Knowledge Management, and Organization Development is explored. The issue of whether or not organizations can actually learn is discussed.

Chapter 6 discusses the number of methods organizations can use to promote workplace learning. Techniques such as making time and space for learning, rewarding learning at the individual and the group level, modeling learning behavior by senior managers, mentoring, and so forth are examined. Practical suggestions for trainers and adult educators on ways to address the need for holistic learning and development are also discussed. Suggestions to help facilitate the transition from training to workplace learning are offered.

In the final chapter I speculate on the future of workplace

learning. There are a number of trends that are affecting organizations that make a focus on training increasingly ineffective. Conversely, technology is making workplace learning more of a reality. Finally, I propose a new kind of workplace learner, the New Era Emancipated Learner, and explore some of his or her future needs.

If this book helps increase the recognition of the need for workplace learning it will be a start. The momentum that has been gained recently will need to be maintained. As individuals and organizations begin to see the benefits of workplace learning such as increased worker commitment, more flexible and rapid responses to change, and improved quality and customer satisfaction, they will become more committed to its use. It is my hope that this book will contribute toward that end.

THE AUTHOR

Robert W. Rowden is an Associate Professor of Adult
Education and Human Resource Development at Florida Atlantic University in Ft Lauderdale/Davie, Florida, USA. He is also
an Adjunct Professor of Human Resources in the OnLine graduate program at Capella University. He received his Ph.D. in
Human Resource Development from Georgia State University.
He also has an MBA with a concentration in Employee Relations
and a B.S. in Applied Science and Technology. Following a
career in the military and law enforcement, he has worked as a
consultant to small businesses in human resource issues, served
as a Vice President of Human Resources in an international firm,
and served as a Training and Organization Development Specialist. After teaching as an adjunct instructor at community and
junior colleges, he took a position as an Assistant Professor in
the School of Continuing Education at Palm Beach Atlantic College in West Palm Beach, FL. He moved to Brenau University in
Gainesville, GA as an Assistant Professor of Human Resources
in the College of Education. Later he moved to Mercer University—Atlanta as an Associate Professor of Human Resources/
Management in the School of Business. He continued with that
assignment until moving to Florida Atlantic University. His current research interests include the relationship between workplace learning and job satisfaction, HRD in small businesses,
strategic leadership, and management and organization development. His most recent works have been published in *Human
Resource Development International, Advanced Management
Journal, Journal of Workplace Learning, Employment Relations
Today, Human Resource Development Quarterly, Leadership and*

*Organization Development Journal, Journal of Business & Entre-
preneurship, Australian Vocation-Educational Review, Business
Journal for Entrepreneurs,* and *New Directions for Adult and
Continuing Education.*

Does a business have an obligation to maintain its employees' intellectual health?

CHAPTER 1
Exploring the Concept

Einstein has been quoted as saying, "The significant problems that we have cannot be solved at the same level of thinking with which we created them" (Kirkwood & Pangarkar, 2003, p. 10). While he was speaking about the state of the world in general, his message is equally important for organizations struggling to be successful in the ever-changing and extremely competitive environment. As the base of the economy changes from manufacturing products to creating and managing knowledge, and as organizations reduce the number of managerial layers, greater knowledge levels and the capacity to develop new skills are expected of more and more employees. Increases in competition, globalization, and the speed of change have helped to highlight the importance of the capacity for lifelong learning in organizations as a key to both survival and success (Dumphy, Turner & Crawford, 1997; Easterby-Smith, Snell & Gehardi, 1998; Fulmer, Gibbs & Keys, 1998; Norris, 2003). Organizations have begun to recognize and promote their human resources as a source of significant and sustainable competitive advantage (Prahalad & Hamel, 1990; Pfeffer, 1998). *Developing the human resources* of a company would seem to be key to increasing production and closing the gap between the level of worker skill and present and future needs. Schein (2003) explains that "all forms of learning and change start with some form of dissatisfaction as frustration generated by data that disconfirms our expectations and hopes" (p. 2). Since the explosion of knowledge and the innovation of technology have drastically changed the characteristics of the workplace, learning becomes the most important factor to survive changes in today's organizations.

In fact, U.S. businesses spend $60 billion a year training their workers (Industry Report, *Training*, 2003). However, recent research suggests that a lot of this money may be wasted because employers focus on training rather than a range of learning opportunities (Billett, 2002; Norris, 2003; Rowden, 1995; Rowden & Ahmed, 2000; Rowden, 2002; and Rowden & Conine, 2004). Leslie, Aring and Brand (1998) found that "learning . . . which may take place inside or outside the classroom—offers the possibility for enhanced workplace productivity" (p. 12). Much of employee development is informal and randomly experienced; in fact, on-the-job learning can occur in a number of different ways—not just in formal training programs. Learning, as opposed to training, is more appropriate to a business environment in which jobs are constantly changing. The capacity to learn is one of the fundamental attributes of human beings and involves them developing and changing as time passes (Arnold, Cooper & Robertson (1995). Therefore, what is needed is a broader reconceptionalization of learning in the workplace.

LEARNING AND TRAINING
ARE NOT SYNONYMOUS

Managers and leaders in organizations often, mistakenly, equate training with learning. Although often used interchangeably, they are distinct concepts. Training tends to concentrate on short-term change for learning a specific task, where learning, by contrast, emphisises the long term and is a continuous process. In addition to building knowledge, skills, and abilities, learning also emphasizes what workers believe they must know, do, or feel to interact with others to achieve results. It aims to spur learners into thinking creatively about their work and understanding their own work style. Training can be a valuable tool in building a learning environment, but is insufficient alone. Learning takes in the total of an individual's acquisition and assimilation of experiences, information, and daily activities.

Training can only provide information. The information can only be converted to knowledge if workers are capable of applying it to their jobs. When the person applies these skills through practice and reinforcement, learning takes place. Training is often viewed as a separate function from the employees' work activity, especially since it requires taking time away from the job. The new skills, knowledge, or abilities are often not integrated or encouraged in the daily activities once the worker returns to the job. This tends to result in training being viewed as simply an expense rather than a useful tool. Learning should be viewed differently.

Learning is an internal process. It can be something that not only takes place in the brain, but can also have an affective and physical component. The process itself cannot always be observed, but the results are often apparent. Learning is defined by Billett (2002) as "a relatively permanent change in behavior, cognition, or affect that occurs as a result of one's interaction with the environment" (p. 56). Several aspects of this definition are important. First, the focal point of learning is change, either by acquiring something new (like skill in conducting meetings), or modifying something that already exists (like a basketball player achieving greater accuracy in shooting a basket). Second, the change must be long lasting before learning has really occurred. If an administrative assistant can recall the commands needed to create a macro operation in a word processing program on the second day of a training course, but cannot remember them four days later back on the job, learning has not occurred. Third, learning can include behavior, affect, or cognition, or any combination of the three. Learning outcomes can be skill-based (climbing a utility pole), cognitive (procedures for applying for a research grant), or affective (becoming more safety conscious). Finally, learning results from an individual's interaction with the environment. Learning does not include behavior changes attributable to physical maturation or a temporary condition (e.g., fatigue or drugs).

Bryans and Smith (2000) elaborate on the idea of learning. They stated that "learning should be seen as a qualitative change in a person's way of seeing, experiencing, understanding, conceptualizing something in the real world—rather than as a quantitative change in the amount of knowledge someone possesses"

(p. 271). This suggests that it is impossible to look at learning in a way that is content- and context-free.

These definitions of learning make it clear that people acquire and develop skills and knowledge, and change as a result of an interaction between forces within the learner and in the environment. Of course the workplace provides an environment rife with learning opportunities. Emphasing learning rather than training, is a better approch for organizations with changing job environments (Marsick & Volpe, 1999).

PHILOSOPHICAL PERSPECTIVES

Over the past several decades, three distinct perspectives on the process by which workers learn to perform their jobs better have emerged. One view that developed very early on during the Industrial Revolution—and still held by many today—is that workers need training and development (T&D) to do their jobs efficiently. Later, beginning in the 1970s, the concept of Human Resource Development (HRD) began to emerge. HRD added Organization Development (OD) and Career Development (CD) to T&D. Recently, the concept of Workplace Learning (WPL) has captivated many who help facilitate worker learning.

DeSimone, Werner and Harris (2002) have defined training as "a short-term change effort that provides employees the knowledge and skills needed to do a particular task or job" (p. 10). Training is intended to improve individual work performance by providing people with the knowledge, skills, and abilities necessary to be successful in their work. The work requirements and expectations of the organization's stakeholders should be used to drive the training process.

Every employee performance problem cannot be solved by training. Some problems can be solved by training, but other problems require management action. According to Toll (1999), only about 10 percent of employee performance problems are attributable to a lack of knowledge, skills, or abilities (KSAs) that can be addressed by training. The other 90 percent of worker performance problems involve the need to change the work environment and must be solved by management.

Problems caused by the organization's work environment can only be solved through management action. After all, all aspects of the work environment are controlled by management—including who will be selected to do the work, what equipment will be used, how workers will be compensated, what goals and standards will they be expected to meet, and what type of feedback will they be given. No amount of training can solve problems caused by poor supervision, poor organizational planning, poor reward systems that reinforce the wrong behaviors or results, or other such work environment problems resulting from management inaction (Kirkwood & Pangarkar, 2003).

Therefore, training that will help people perform their work should be grounded in a thorough understanding of the work they do and the unique corporate culture in which that work is carried out. Ideally, training is tightly focused on giving people just what they need to be successful in their particular corporate culture.

Human Resource Development (HRD), broadly defined, is about developing the work-related capabilities of people; people working as individuals, in teams, and in organizations. HRD is about providing people with the opportunity to acquire knowledge, understanding, skills, and conducting training that enables them to perform effectively. HRD encompasses staff development and training, continuing professional development/continuing professional education, and workplace learning (Walton, 1999).

For the most part, HRD researchers have paid more attention to studying trainers in organizations than to learners. Organizations hire, promote, or transfer many people into HRD or trainer roles, and have a need to find efficient ways to orient, train, and develop them. Organizations are always looking for bench marking or "best practices" to improve their operation, especially HRD. Examples of "successful" practices which empower or make one's organization seem "exemplary" or ingenious are prevalent. Perhaps such themes attract a greater likelihood of funding from both internal and external sources. Academic institutions require a foundation for curricula on which to build academic programs intended to help people enter or advance in the field. According to the American Society for Training and Development (ASTD) there are about 300 graduate programs that meet those needs. (Norris, 2003).

The results of this is that much research has been done on what roles trainers should play, what type of outputs they should produce, and what competencies they should possess. More than 30 years of research has been devoted to clarifying the roles and competencies of practitioners in a field often referred to as Training and Development (T&D), Performance Improvement (PI), HRD, and Workplace Learning. However, while ASTD [which interestingly still identifies itself in terms of *training and development*], has been sponsoring research on the role of practitioners, no like-agency has sponsored or conducted research on the roles or competencies of learners. Clearly, the trainer's role is important and will remain an integral part of the organization, but the learner's role is of equal or greater importance. What the learner does—or does not do—affects every aspect of the organization.

Workplace learning refers to learning that occurs during the activities and experiences of work. Fenwick (2001, p. 4) offers that workplace learning is "to imply human change or growth that occurs primarily in activities and context of work." It can include some type of structured formal class or presentation where the learning outcomes are geared to accomplish organizational goals. Workplace learning may also include learning activities such as on-the-job training, mentoring, or coaching for performance. Invariably, workplace learning describes the social interaction between people, people in groups, and groups across boundaries.

Realizing the importance of worker competence in the new economy, organizations are spending billions of dollars every year on employee development in their quest for competitive advantage (Kirkwood & Pangarkar, 2003). In spite of this expensive approach to training, most learning takes place in the everyday activities of work (Marsick & Watkins, 1990;

Rowden, 2002). It has been known for some time that more learning occurs in the workplace than just what happens in formal training classrooms.

Watkins and Marsick (1992) have identified the different forms of workplace learning as formal, informal, and incidental.3 Formal learning (training), of course, is discrete planned events (experiences) used to instruct people how to perform specific defined jobs. It is typically institutionally sponsored and highly structured. Informal learning may occur in institutions, but is not typically classroom-based or highly structured, and control of learning is in the hands of the learner not the organization. Formal learning includes both an expressed organization goal and a defined process. Informal learning can occur whether or not there is an expressed goal and can serve individual as well as corporate objectives. For example, informal learning might best occur when a coworker shows a new employee how to use a machine through an actual demonstration rather than through a classroom presentation.

Although interconnected, informal and incidental learning are not necessarily the same. Incidental learning occurs as an unintended by-product of some other activity such as trial-and-error experimentation or interpersonal interaction. The intention of the activity is task accomplishment but serendipitously increases particular knowledge, skills, or understanding. People are not always conscious of it, but incidental learning almost always takes place. Marsick and Volpe (1999) extend the understanding of the need to learn continuously through both formal and informal means to enhance organizational effectiveness. Formal and informal learning tend to be intentional whereas incidental learning is not.

While informal and incidental learning occur as part of everyday work processes and activities and produces mainly implicit or tacit knowledge, formal learning takes place in the context of organized training and learning activities and is meant to generate explicit and formal knowledge and skills. Given the important role that they have in organizations, informal and incidental learning and the tacit knowledge which arises as a result of the unplanned and often hidden types of learning, need to be put to use in practices intended to promote worker development

It is interesting to review what is known about organizational learning (T&D, HRD, and WPL). The differences among the philosophical perspectives are greater than merely providing new labels for old ideas. Understanding what is known about them is essential to understanding the need for similar knowledge about the role and competencies of workplace learners.

COMPARING T&D, HRD, AND WORKPLACE LEARNING

To best understand the distinctions among training and development (T&D), human resource development (HRD), and workplace learning (WPL), it is useful to further examine the elements of each. In addition to the definitions, what are the assumptions of each?—the goals?—the relationship between the trainer/facilitator and the learners?—the principles that drive learning?—what motivates learning?—and the guiding models?—the role of the learner? Highlighting the differences will help underscore the importance of committing to the holistic process of learning, rather than training.

As previously stated, Training and Development (T&D) has planned learning interventions at its center. Key competencies are identified and formal training is developed that enables employees to perform their current jobs. Human Resource Development (HRD) is "the integrated use of training and development, organization development, and career development to improve individual, group, and organizational effectiveness" (McLagan, 1989, p. 7) to enable employees to better perform their current and future jobs. Workplace learning is the way in which workers, or groups of workers acquire, interpret, assimilate, or reorganize related clusters of facts, skills, and feelings, and how they construct meaning from their personal and shared organizational life.

Another distinction among the three concepts can be made

based on what assumptions are made about people. Corporate trainers who subscribe to the tenets of T&D generally believe that people need and want to be instructed about their job. HRD believes that people should be considered self-actualizing and that learning is key to self-actualization. Workplace learning, on the other hand, holds that people want to learn and develop and they see learning as a way to achieve their potential and reach their goals. Organizational success is best achieved when there is a close alignment between organizational goals and individual goals.

Some distinctions can be made in terms of the main purpose or goal of each philosophy. T&D has as its main goal or purpose to improve knowledge, skills, and abilities about the job. HRD is concerned with the integration of training and development, organization development, and career development for the purpose of improved performance through planned learning. Workplace learning holds with each of these goals, but places the emphasis on the worker as learner. The worker is often in the best position to know what needs to be learned and what is the best way to go about learning it. These different beliefs tend to drive the learning in the organizations. Organizations with a philosophy of T&D believe that the individual job performance should be the purpose of learning. Immediate results should be obvious from training, and it should be readily apparent how those results relate to the job. HRD, on the other hand, holds the principles that greater organizational effectiveness will be the result of increased worker skills and knowledge about a particular set of tasks. HRD looks to join learning at the individual level (training) with group and organizational interventions (OD) to better facilitate learning, and development (CD). Workplace learning believes that providing an environment of continuous learning is critical to individual and organizational performance. Workplace learning incorporates the issues of individual and organizational learning as sets of practices that occur both formally and informally within organizations. The workplace learning philosophy highlights the complex and context-specific nature of learning.

Perhaps the area of greatest distinction among the three

perspectives lies in the view of the relationship between the trainer (facilitator) and trainee (learner). Training and Development focuses on making people productive in their jobs. Training tries to accomplish that purpose through a short-term perspective; the development component seeks the same purpose with a longer-term goal. The main emphasis is on determining the knowledge, skills, and abilities that are crucial to job success, and then building the individual *knowledge, skills, and abilities* (KSAs) in line with those expectations. As a result, the relationship between the *trainer* and the *trainee* relies on the traditional teacher-student model. That is, the trainer (teacher) is responsible for the task of teaching the trainee (student) what she or he must know, do, or accomplish to be successful on the job.

Human Resource Development uses an integrated approach to achieve change through planned instruction. It blends the individual focused short-term learning initiative of training with organization development learning initiatives at the group level, along with longer-term career development learning initiatives that center on the work requirements of the future. Since the sole purpose of HRD is not just training, the relationship between the trainer and the trainee is complex. The relationship will depend of the exact type of intervention. If individual training or group learning (OD) is the purpose of the interaction, then the interaction is likely to be that of the teacher-student as with T&D. If, however, the emphasis is longer-term in scope, the interaction is likely to be more of a mentor-mentee relationship. In the end, HRD is still responsible for teaching the worker the necessary skills to be successful on the job.

Workplace learning does not have training as its sole option. The worker does have a major role in planning instruction, and even more importantly, in identifying ways to support and encourage learning. All stakeholders in the organization can have a role to play in the effort. The Workplace Learning practitioner serves as an enabler, a resource, and a learning specialist. He or she facilitates the process but does not take sole ownership and responsibility for it. The learners are the ones who take responsibility for pursuing their own learning initiatives. In Workplace Learning, the practitioner functions as a facilitator and works as a partner with the worker in the learning quest.

T&D are management responsibilities because it is management's job to ensure that workers can perform their jobs properly. Employees are motivated to learn because they want to be successful in performing their jobs in keeping with management's requirements. In HRD, learning is motivated by individual motivation to learn through training, individual motivation to work effectively in groups, and individual motivation to prepare for future career advancement. With Workplace Learning, organizations sponsor learning because they are aware of the competitive importance of workers. Individuals are motivated to learn in response to present work needs or future career goals. Learning is *work* focused rather than *job* focused because jobs may go away but meaningful work seldom does.

As a field of study, T&D has planned learning events at its core while the field of HRD concepts on the three-fold purposes of giving individuals the knowledge and skills they need to perform, helping them formulate and realize career goals, and interacting effectively in groups. The many facets of workplace learning concentrate on progressive change in the workplace though learning strategies. The primary model that provides guidance for the field of T&D is instructional systems design (ISD). The field of HRD utilizes the ISD model as well, but also incorporates the action research model, and various career development models. The models that guide the field of Workplace Learning would best be described as that of adult learning and andragogy from the Adult Education model. Table 1 is a summary of the three perspectives.

LEARNING AS A *PROCESS*, NOT A *PRODUCT*

The current predominant view of learning in organizations favored by T&D practitioners and many HRD practitioners regards the mind as a container and knowledge as a type of substance to be deposited in the container (Lakoff & Johnson,

Table 1. Comparison of T&D, HRD, & Workplace Learning

	T & D	HRD	WORKPLACE LEARNING
DEFINITION	formal training to perform current jobs	integrated use of T&D, OD, & CD at all levels to enable employees to better perform their current and future jobs	use of multiple learning strategies, and meaning-making in personal and shared organizational life
ASSUMPTIONS	people need and want to be instructed about their job	people considered self-actualizing and learning key to self-actualization	people want to learn and develop, and achieve individual and organizational goals
PURPOSE	to improve knowledge, skills, and abilities about the job	improved performance through planned learning	focus on the worker as learner believing that the worker is best at identifying learning needs.
BELIEFS ABOUT LEARNING	individual job performance should be focus of learning and results relate back to the job	organizational effectiveness results of increased worker skills and knowledge about a particular set of tasks	environment of continuous learning critical to performance, and highlights context-specific nature of learning
RELATIONSHIP	traditional teacher-student model	if individual training or group learning (OD), teacher-student—if longer-term focus (CD) more mentor-mentee	learner-centered; facilitator
MOTIVATION	management driven—employees motivated to learn because they want to be successful in performing their jobs in keeping with management's requirements	individual motivation to learn through training, to work effectively in groups, and individual motivation to prepare for future career advancement	organizations sponsor learning because they are aware of the competitive importance of workers; individuals motivated to learn in response to present work needs or future career goals

Table 1. (Continued)

FIELD OF PRACTICE	planned learning events	giving individuals the knowledge and skills they need to perform, formulate and realize career goals, and interact effectively in groups	progressive change in the workplace though learning strategies
MODELS	instructional systems design (ISD)	utilizes ISD model, but also incorporate the action research model, and various career development models	best described as that of adult learning and andragogy from the Adult Education model

1980). Bereiter states that "under the mind-as-container metaphor, knowledge is treated as consisting of objects contained in individual minds, something like the contents of mental filing cabinets (2002, p. 179). The focus on adding more "substance" to the mind emphasizes the products of learning.

Many policies and practices that directly impact learning at work are rooted in the learning-as-product view. For example, the emphasis on competency-based training from the Performance Improvement perspective views work performance as a series of decontextualized minute elements, which workers are thought of as needing to pick up one by one (Billett, 2002). After the discrete element is acquired, application or transfer to future circumstances by the learner is assumed to be unproblematic. This learning-as-product approach is also used when generic skills, such as problem solving and communication, are presented as discrete, decontextualized elements that, once acquired, can simply be transferred to diverse situations.

The learning-as-product view involves two basic assumptions. The **stability assumption** believes the products of learning to be relatively stable over time. This stability enables learning to be incorporated into training programs, passed on from trainer to worker, and the attainment of the discrete elements to be measured in examinations. Garrick (1998) puts this assumption of what he calls *standard theories of learning* as "a self-

evident presupposition that the knowledge or skill to be acquired is itself stable and reasonably well-defined" (p. 137).
There is also a **replicability assumption** that learning can be
literally the same for different learners. This matter is reflected
in the statement that trainees are said to have the same "attainment"—something like two containers being filled with identi-
cal substances.

However, workers today must be able to handle unfamil-
iar situations in this rapidly changing world—with ease. It is
difficult to predict what knowledge, skills, and abilities may be
necessary in the future, therefore workers need to understand
and apply processes which enable them to acquire KSAs as
needed. In other words, they need to *learn how to learn*. Using
a process-oriented approach, organizations can engage workers
in activities which require them to think, communicate, organize, interact, make decisions, and solve problems. In this way,
workers take control of their own learning and can apply a
variety of learning processes.

Learning is a social phenomenon; people of all ages learn
from and with each other. Organizations can maximize learning
opportunities by encouraging workers to work together in
pairs, in groups, and in training classes, or by implementing
programs such as peer tutoring or mentorships. Interactive learning reinforces important processes, such as communicating and
problem solving. As well, it encourages workers to function as
cooperating, rather than competing, members of groups and
enables them to take more responsibility for their own learning
at work.

Workers themselves are the most significant of all the
organizational stakeholders, and their needs should be the key
determinants of the learning process. Experiences prior to coming to the current company determine what they bring with
them. Organizations can build on those experiences by bringing
the world of the learner into the organization and extending
learning beyond the training room walls. For each worker, those
experiences, strengths, and needs may be quite different. Organizations need to recognize and respond to workers as individuals, while remaining cognizant of the importance of the goals of

the organization. Responding to workers as individuals requires process-centered learning, that is, learning which is shaped by the needs of the learner. The process model conceives of workplace learning

> in terms of its processes rather than its products, and must be approached and planned by reference to the kinds of activities and experiences that constitute it, rather than to the outcomes it is hoped it will lead to . . . the major emphasis is on the processes of development it sets out to promote, so that it can be said to be concerned with products or outcomes, these will be defined in terms of intellectual development and cognitive functioning rather than in terms of quantities of knowledge absorbed or changes of behavioral performance. (Blenkin & Kelly, 1981, p. 89)

A process model focuses on providing opportunity for experiences which offer intellectual challenge through thinking tasks and problem solving without identifying singular outcomes. In teaching information skills within a process model, workers are encouraged to actively engage in information rather than to listen unquestioningly as they receive the knowledge of others. Not only do workers learn by doing, they also need to reflect on the learning process itself so that when a situation arises where information skills are called for, they can create a plan to address their needs drawing on their own understanding of previous knowledge and interpretation. In this way, they take control of the learning process and are able to transfer their skills from one situation to another. The relationship of the learner to the information source is direct whereby worker learning is a personal interpretation rather than translation of the trainer's experience. Learners construct their own framework of understanding to make meaning of a subject and convert it into personal knowledge. This kind of internal processing encourages the use of metacognition whereby workers question what they need to know and identify the means to obtain needed information.

An example of teaching knowledge, skills, and abilities

examplly

using the process model is problem solving that is at least partly initiated by the workers as a result of interest in a problem. This requires that workers identify and interpret information to produce knowledge for themselves. They must identify what they need to know and how they will search for what they need. It draws on their own experience and information-handling experience and exposes the process of assessing the problem, finding and interpreting, and suggesting solutions as equally important. Information skills are exposed as essential learning tools in the quest for solutions to the problem and find obvious merit in part of the thinking process. False starts, wrong turns, and unsubstantiated conclusions are legitimate pathways and acceptable behaviors because they mirror true active learning as it shapes new ways of thinking. *helps abate fear of failure*

The best way to integrate the process model is through integrated learning rather than individual training classes because the former is more likely to foster the view that information skills are generic learning tools and are connected across all situations. Trainers who value process learning emphasize *how* workers learn to find out about a situation as much as *what* they eventually discover about the subject material itself. Workers who are involved with creating personal meaning are engaged in finding information, reading, taking notes, discussing ideas, and presenting their findings to coworkers. On a daily basis, they discuss how they learn the necessary skills and strategies that make them successful self-directed learners. In effect, they think about how they think and learn, openly analyze problems they have in completing a task, and take charge of mapping out alternative strategies that will help them accomplish it.

This type of learning provides a framework for the articulation of the learning process throughout the organization because it involves researching topics. Moving the process of investigation into daily activities identifies it as an important part of learning and consequently elevates the nature of the process in the minds of workers. Presenting questions and topics to be explored rather than distributing packaged training serves as an enormous stimulus to provoke inquiring minds into

seems very ideal —.
what is their motivation?

thought and action. Workers are encouraged to discover and
reinvent for themselves the very information they need to learn.
This active participation makes learning meaningful and memo-
rable because it becomes a personal voyage of discovery as
opposed to a trainer-manufactured workshop of information. An
effective learning process enables workers to develop the necessary knowledge, skills, and abilities to enable them to cope
with the challenges which they face now and in the future.

True but, super idealistic.

CONCLUSION

The increasingly competitive nature of the economy, combined with the demographic, occupational, and workplace
changes, have had a significant impact on the nature of the
workplace itself. These changes have meant that the skill level
of employees must be continuously cultivated and developed
in order to keep up with the demands of today's businesses.
The skill mix required is ever-changing with the advent of the
latest technology, with employers demanding complex skills
such as communication and problem-solving skills, in addition
to technical skills.

Although most will agree that the changing workplace
requires ever-changing skills and knowledge, not everyone
agrees on the best approach to meeting the challenge. The
older notion of training, or formal learning, is still prevalent
today. Even as T&D has expanded its role into HRD, the primary emphasis is still on training. While training still has its
place, most will agree that it is insufficient today. A new, broader
view of the learning process at work is needed. Learning can
no longer be viewed as just occurring during special classes and
workshops. Learning needs to shift from the mastery of discrete
topics to learning-how-to-learn, learning about self and others,
and learning about work groups and the organization.

This type of learning does not depend on the teacher or
expert since learning is a social construct and learning occurs in
groups of coworkers as they construct and reconstruct knowledge, skills, and abilities. Real organizational learning occurs

when workers solve difficult problems that the formal system does not address. The lack of classroom knowledge being used back on the job (transfer of training) will no longer be an issue since learning happens during work interactions. (This holistic view of learning allows workers to focus on the self-organizing and self-directed nature of organizational learning.)

The increased emphasis on the importance of workplace learning is welcomed by workers and organizations alike. It saves the business time and money to have the learning occur where people are, rather than them having to go to it. It allows the worker control over their own learning and development. Work and learning go hand-in-hand as totally complementary activities. In fact, whether an activity is called "working" or not, it generates experiences—and experiences are the staple diet of learning. Working is learning and learning happens at and through work. Once this is understood, the next important step is to create a work environment conducive to learning.

CHAPTER 2
Environmental Factors

There is little question that the knowledge individuals bring to bear on the work they do represents the new currency in the global economy (Billett, 2001; Garrick, 1999). Central to organizational success is an appreciation of the skills and processes involved in the application, communication, development, and retention of knowledge in the workplace. An organization that values collaboration and learning is a prerequisite for success (Fulmer, Gibbs, & Keys, 1998).

In the current economic times, more emphasis is being placed on the importance of the intellectual assets, that is, the knowledge workers have about what they do. Many organizations feel the only way to survive and prosper in a world characterized by speed, complexity, global competition, down-sizing, and constant change, is to work smarter, not harder. According to Bennis (1997) and Wellins (1991) the key to working smarter is to collaborate with one another. According to them and others, collaborating and exchanging knowledge with colleagues on a regular basis is likely to result in a situation where what can be achieved by the group as a whole is greater than the sum of what can be achieved as individuals working alone. Von Krogh, Ichijo, and Nonaka's (2000) observations of "learning-aware" companies led them to conclude that systematically exchanging what is known with one another can result in faster knowledge creation and innovation, more efficient and effective use of existing organizational know-how, reduced risk of loss of valuable knowledge when people leave the organization, and better understanding of customers and clients including anticipating their needs. They also believe that promoting learning for improved individual and organizational performance requires a set of organizational activities specifically designed to facilitate or enable the creation of new knowledge, the exchange of existing organizational knowledge, and the retention of lessons learned from experiences at work. The workplace environment cannot be discounted as an important component in the success of Workplace Learning.

After accepting that Workplace Learning is a more inclusive way to conceptualize the learning that goes on in organizations, there are a number of other things that need to be attended to in order to foster that learning. Among them are environmental factors. Environmental factors include both *internal* and *external* elements that influence workplace learning. Among the internal factors are the organization's climate and culture, managerial support, and communication patterns. External factors can include such things as "globalization," outsourcing, competition and emerging markets, and the changing concept of meaningful work. Maintaining a holistic view of an organization as a learning environment is much more complicated than just offering some training classes and hoping the training will fill the learning needs of the workers.

ORGANIZATIONAL INTERNAL ENVIRONMENT

Everyone is very much aware of the effect the environment has on daily life. Spirits soar when the sun is shining, the sky is blue, and a gentle breeze is blowing. Conversely, when it's cold, rainy, and gray it is very easy to feel depressed and down. The environment of an organization can have the same impact on the workplace. When considering the environment in which learning experiences take place, however, it is important to think not only about the physical needs of the workers, but also psychological and social needs. Therefore, it is important to consider the environment in its broadest sense, including not only the physical environment of the learning space, but also the physical, social, and emotional "environment" that the learner brings to the learning endeavor.

There are a number of components to the organization's internal environment. Some of the components are the management systems, the employees, the organizational climate, the board of directors, organizational structure, owners and stakeholders, and culture, to name a few (Jones, 1981). If organizations are to successfully develop environments that promote workplace learning, fundamental components of organizational life should be examined and analyzed. The main components of the internal environment discussed here are culture, climate, structure, and leadership.

Culture

While some people use the terms culture and climate interchangeably, they are just as distinct and separate in the organizational "world" as they are on planet Earth. Corporate culture is related to climate but is a separate concept. Culture is the pattern of beliefs and values, rituals, assumptions, norms, artifacts, and patterns of behavior that are shared by the members of the organization. Schein (2003, p. 12) has defined organizational culture as

> a pattern of shared basic assumptions that the group learned as it solved its problems of external adaptation and internal integration, that has worked well enough to be considered valid, and, therefore, to be taught to new members as the correct way to perceive, think and feel in relation to those problems.

Culture is based on the organization's experience about what to do, what not to do, what is worth doing, how people should interact, how decisions are made, how recognition takes place, who gets promoted, and how the organization reacts to the external environment. It influences the actions of all individuals and groups within the organization. It is important to have a thorough understanding of the culture in the organization (West, 1994).

Climate

Organizational climate, on the other hand, is a function of variables such as organizational personality, hopes, attitudes, biases, feeling tones, and organizational mood which ultimately establish the working environment. It is this environment which defines the informal rules for employees regarding their individual and collective behavior and their beliefs about how they are expected to treat each other, relate to their superiors, treat customers, suppliers, competitors and other critical stakeholders. Altmann (2000) explains,

> At its most basic level, organizational climate refers to employee perceptions of the work environment. Generally, these perceptions are descriptively based rather than value based. . . . organizational climate is more than simply a summary of employee likes and dislikes. (p. 62)

Climate is bound by perception, which may not always correspond to organizational facts, but nonetheless comprise reality in the eyes of employees. Numerous climates can exist, depending on what facet of the organization is being described. There are, however, certain climate types which are common across a number of different organizations and industries. Examples include climates of fairness, safety, support, communication, tolerance for risk, flexibility, and continuous learning. Climate is related to employee behavior, organizational outcomes, and management leadership style, and as such, is an important factor to consider. For example, an organization can have a climate of fairness, support, and open communication, along with high pay scales—a good climate. At the same time, that organization can have a culture that expects long hours, hard work, and total dedication. Culture is "the way we do things around here," climate is how the workers feel about the workplace.

Structure

Structure and design significantly influence an organization's ability to adapt to new situations. Organizational structure can inhibit or foster creativity, innovation, communication, and learning. The problem with organizational structure though, is that it is the result of many factors, including history, organic growth, strategy, operational design, product diversity, logistics, marketing, client base, supplier base and so forth (James, James, & Ashe, 1990). There are many definitions of types of organizational structure. Blackler and McDonald (2000) identify two common ones: 1) mechanistic structures include centralized control and authority, clearly defined tasks, vertical communication links, obedience to supervisors, rigidity and inflexibility, and 2) organic structures include decentralization of authority, tasks loosely defined, horizontal communications, greater individual authority, flexible, adaptable. However, Blackler and McDonald caution that the above can be misleading. For example, flat organizations are generally preferred and hierarchical ones not preferred; however, even flat organizations are in reality hierarchical, as they maintain the same structure, control, and rigidity—just with fewer levels.

Despite the changes in organizations with the move toward more organic through the flattening of the structure, introduction of new technology, and so forth, most work environments in the United States today still conform to a hierarchical, bureaucratic pattern. A number of studies have indicated that there is less motivation for self-improvement and more blocks to learning in traditional, hierarchically structured organizations than in open systems that are organized around purposes—not preordained centers of power (see for example: Altmann, 2000; Bennis, 1997; Toll, 1999; Wellins, 1991). The structure of the organization determines the distribution of power, the control systems, the reward systems, the information systems, and the communication process. Policies, rules, and procedures that fuel distrust and encourage mediocrity may develop in hierarchical, bureaucratic structures. In addition, artificial barriers constructed by a pyramid design tend to stifle authentic communication between people (James, James, & Ashe, 1990). Thus, hierarchical, bureaucratic organizations may have limited capacity for nurturing the development of individual members and the whole system.

Leadership

Along with culture, climate, and structure, leadership has tremendous influence on an organization's ability to foster learning. Although leadership has been of interest to society for thousands of years, research into leadership only began in the early part of the twentieth century. Research on leadership has taken several approaches. Most of the research can be classified into one of four major categories: trait approaches, situational approaches, power-influence approaches, and behavioral approaches (Yukl, 1994). Mixed results have been attained in attempting to improve the effectiveness of leaders. No one method has been found to be very effective in every situation (Bass, 1990; Yukl, 1994). Leadership is defined by Rowden (2000) as "the behavior of an individual that results in non-coercive influence when that person is directing and coordinating the activities of a group toward the accomplishment of a shared goal (p. 30).

Leaders carry out this process by applying their leadership attributes, such as beliefs, values, ethics, character, knowledge, and skills. Although the position as a manager, supervisor, leader, etc. comes with the authority to accomplish certain tasks and objectives in the organization, this power does not make a person a leader . . . it simply makes her or him the boss. Providing leadership differs in that it makes the followers *want* to achieve high goals, rather than simply bossing people around. Controlling behavior stems from the assumption that workers are immature and dependent. The feeling is, therefore, that leaders must keep tight hold on the reins, make all decisions, and avoid risks whenever possible (Peled, 2000).

Very little has been written on the role leaders play in making (or breaking) workplace learning. However, the general leadership literature does provide four explanations as to why some leaders are successful, and others are not, that may shed light on the situation. The "psychology first" school of thought focuses on personality to explain why some leaders are successful. Yukl (1994) anchored the success of leaders in their psychological need to manage others, their quest for power, and their capacity for empathy. The "strategy first" school of thought argues that successful leaders act as great analytic statesmen. Porter (1990, p. 615) states that true leaders "set strategy to enhance and extend" the competitive advantage of their organizations. The "human relations first" school of thought focuses on how successful leaders interact with others. Bass (1990) and Peters and Waterman (1984) argued that successful leaders give meaning to the daily routines of their teams by shaping and promoting a new set of values. He argued that successful leaders are above all educators and institution-builders who convey excitement to their employees. The "organization first" school of thought argues that every manager has the potential to become successful when provided with the proper organizational support. Tulgan (2002) believes that successful managers work in "organizations where the culture fosters collaboration and teamwork and where structures encourage people to 'do the right thing'" (p. 184). The opportunities and incentives for problem solving are created by organizations which encourage the free flow of information, create overlapping responsibilities that encourage workers to promote their own ideas, facilitate cross-functional exchanges, and build good learning environments (Tulgan, 2002). But, as important as these factors are, they fail to capture the whole picture of successful leadership.

Culture, climate, structure, and leadership reinforce one another. The axiom, "you tend to manage the way you are managed," appropriately describes the vicious cycle that too often occurs in organizations. If organizational life is to become a matter of releasing people's creative energies, not controlling their behavior, then all four internal environmental variables will have to support workplace learning. Of course, what goes on outside the organization, itself, can impact how an organization functions.

ORGANIZATIONAL EXTERNAL ENVIRONMENT

An organization's *external environment* includes many elements outside the boundary of the organization. This complex external environment can be divided into two sectors—the General Environment and the Task Environment. The General Sector contains such components as the political/legal environment, economic forces, the natural environment, technological forces, sociocultural forces, and the international/global forces. The Task Sector (or Domain) contains such components as the customers, competitors, suppliers, the labor supply, regulators, and partners. Some components such as environmental complexity and stability can span both sectors (Griffin, Ebert, & Starke, 2005; Jones, 1981). These distinctions are generally true whether the organization is a for-profit concern, not-for-profit, non-profit, or governmental agency (including school systems). All organizations have to acknowledge their environments.

Further, environmental complexity is the number and dissimilarity of external elements relevant to an organization's operations. An environment is considered complex when the task environment has a large number of dissimilar elements. An environment is considered simple when it has a smaller number of dissimilar elements (West, 1994). A telecommunications company is an example of a company facing a complex environment, while a small hardware store is a company facing a simple environment. Environmental stability is the extent and predictability of change in the external elements relevant to an organization's operations. It can be described as either stable or unstable. An environment is considered stable if its elements remain the same or change slowly or predictably. An environment is considered unstable (or dynamic) if it changes frequently or unpredictably (Griffin, et al., 2005). Companies in the microprocessor industry face a very complex and unstable environment. Companies must be aware of the type of environment they face, and to be successful they must respond and adapt to these environmental challenges.

As can be seen, the external environment of an organization can be very complex, and space does not permit a thorough discussion of all aspects of the external environment. However, there are several issues in the external environment that impact workplace learning and those specific components will be explored further. The ones that seem to have the most significance today are "globalization" with its resultant job outsourcing, and sociocultural issues.

Globalization

According to Castka, Bamber, and Sharppe (2003), globalization is "a process of interaction and integration among the people, companies, and governments of different nations, a process driven by international trade and investment and aided by information technology" (p. 149). They assert that this process has effects on the environment, on culture, on political systems, on economic development and prosperity, and on human physical well-being in societies around the world.

However, globalization is not new. For centuries, people and enterprises have been buying from, and selling to, each other in countries widely dispersed. "Foreign trade" existed as far back as the famed Silk Road across Central Asia that connected China and Europe during the Middle Ages. Certainly, people and corporations have invested in enterprises in other countries for a long time. In fact, many of the features of the current wave of globalization are similar to those prevailing before the outbreak of World War I. Policy and technological developments of the past few decades have spurred increases in cross-border trade, investment, and migration large enough to signal a new phase of economic development. For example, since 1950 the volume of world trade has increased by 20 times, and from just 1997 to 1999 foreign investment has nearly doubled, from $468 billion to $827 billion. This current wave of globalization is certainly faster and more pervasive than earlier ones (Marques, 2005).

This process has been driven by policies that have opened economies domestically and internationally. Many governments have adopted free-market economic systems, negotiated dramatic reductions in barriers to commerce, and have established international agreements to promote trade in goods, services, and investments. A defining feature of globalization, therefore, is an international industrial and financial business structure. Technology has been the other principal driver of globalization. Advances in information technology, in particular, have dramatically transformed economic life. Information technologies have provided all sorts of valuable new tools for identifying and pursuing economic opportunities, including faster and more informed analysis of economic trends around the world, easy transfers of assets, and collaboration with far-flung partners (Castka, et al, 2003).

Globalization is deeply controversial, however. Proponents of globalization argue that it allows poor countries and their citizens to develop economically and raise their standards of living, while opponents of globalization claim that the creation of an unfettered international free market has benefited multinational corporations in the Western world at the expense of local enterprises, local cultures, and common people. Resistance to globalization has therefore taken shape both at a popular and at a governmental level as people and governments try to manage the flow of capital, labor, goods, and ideas that constitute globalization (Evans, 2005).

One of the more controversial aspects of globalization is the **outsourcing of jobs**, or what is euphemistically called Business Process Outsourcing (BPO). BPO is "the process of leveraging technology vendors in various third world or developing nations for doing a job which was once the responsibility of the organization" (Singh, 2005, p. 2). Or more simply put, it is shifting an internal job to an outside/external company which might have a completely different geographical location. Examples of jobs outsourced might be customer relations management, customer call centers, telemarketing, payroll maintenance, and finance/accounting management, among others. By outsourcing, companies can increase productivity, cut operational costs, provide customer service, beat the competition, and, in turn, concentrate on their main operations—or so the story goes.

Although many economist see BPO as a win-win situation,

that is not always the case. Outsourcing has a lot of downsides. One of the major downsides of outsourcing is the lack of policies in first-world nations like the United States and the United Kingdom With a lack of policies, each organization is on-its-own and is forced to believe that everything will work out for the best. There is no recourse if it doesn't. Another downside is that with outsourcing, jobs are sure to go. While third world nations benefit, employees in developed countries are increasingly concerned about the number of jobs being moved to places like India, Ireland, China, and Thailand. Many fear that the huge number of jobs that are vanishing from traditional workplaces will spell the elimination of many employment opportunities. Though this perspective may be a bit of a stretch, thousands of jobs that had been performed in the United States, England, Australia, Germany, and other places have been moved to countries with considerably lower wage rates (Evans, 2005).

On balance, this shift is purported to be good for the economies of developed countries, since employers are able to get more accomplished for less, freeing resources for other uses—like creating more jobs, which though different, can be performed by their existing workers. Singh (2005) believes that these new jobs will contribute to corporate success. Employers are evaluating where jobs should be performed most efficiently and cost-effectively. As this evaluation proceeds, there will be even more transnational job movement. However, this movement is not just a matter of economics, as the new location must have a knowledgeable workforce, or the capacity to cost-effectively develop enough people.

The key to career development will be workplace learning. Although some will claim that this support should be provided by governments, it is more likely that employers will offer the growth opportunities to attract and hold the people they will need. Once again, these learning opportunities will draw candidates to join one company, rather than its competitors. The movement of jobs and services across boundaries that globalization has fostered, create further challenges for organizations in dealing with the diverse sociocultural dimensions of the workforce.

Sociocultural Forces

With all the movement of goods, services, and people brought on by globalization comes another challenge for organizations—a multinational workforce. This increased diversity means the bringing together of cultures from all parts of the world. For example, Lien (2004, p. 29) shares some interesting statistics about the U.S. Currently, people of color, women, and immigrants account for 85% of the net growth of the nation's labor force; by 2010, women will be 49% of the labor force; during the 1990s immigrants accounted for 1/3 of the total United States population growth; 35-54 year olds will increase from 38% to 55% from 1985 to 2005; over the next 20 years the U.S. population will grow by 44 million, and Hispanics will account for 47% of the growth, Blacks 22%, Asians 18%, and Whites 13%; persons with physical and mental impairments comprise the single largest "minority" (approximately 45 million individuals), Miami is 2/3 Hispanic, San Francisco is 1/3 Asian American, and by the year 2010, English will be the second language in California.

As is evident, national culture is not the only type of culture that influences managerial and work behavior. Rather, the workplace is influenced by different levels of culture ranging from the supranational (regional, ethnic, religious, linguistic) level through the national, professional, and organizational levels to the group level (Karahanna, Evanisto, & Srite, 2005). This blending of cultures creates a diverse workforce the likes of which have never been seen before, meaning organizations will have to learn to deal with the diversity.

However, a great deal of confusion exists about what diversity is. Marques (2005, p. 283) defines diversity as "the condition of having distinct or unlike elements." In a workplace, this means the variety among people relate to such factors as national origin, but also age, culture, education, employee status, gender, family status, function, physical appearance, race, regional origin, religion, sexual orientation, and thinking style. Though these differences themselves are undeniable, corporations and society at large often deny them by recognizing and valuing only a narrow range of differences. Although these differences have often been ignored or devalued in the past, awareness of the role they play in organizational effectiveness has more recently put the spotlight on diversity. Valuing diversity means acknowledging that other people, other races, other voices, and other cultures have as much integrity and as much claim on the world as anyone else. It is the recognition that there are other ways of seeing the world, solving problems, and working together.

Recognizing diversity means promoting inclusion, creating an environment where all differences are valued, and in which each employee can develop to her or his full potential. From a business perspective, acknowledging diversity is valuable because it means an organization gets the most from its employees. Companies that effectively acknowledge diversity recognize that it is not enough to hire employees from underrepresented groups; they must also provide an environment where all employees are supported and valued (Lien, 2003). Taking all these internal and external environmental factors into account will take an extraordinary effort on the part of organizations to promote workplace learning.

DEVELOPING A LEARNING CLIMATE

As can be seen, changes in the internal and external environments have permanently altered the landscape, with increased automation, erosion of jobs, and more competitive markets. Quite often, organizations' climates and cultures continue to retain legacy beliefs and paradigms derived from previous eras. In fact, many in the workforce today do not understand the new business realities and the need for change, resulting in misemployment and even adversarial workplace cultures. For many businesses, their existing workforce relationships simply create below average productivity, poor safety cultures, reduced profits, and a poor learning environment (Norris, 2003).

Given the environments in which they operate, modern organizations will, by necessity, have to become planned climates of learning. Argysis and Schon (1978) realized some time ago that for organizations to adapt to their environment they need to be perceived as institutions for problem solving and learning. Furthermore, the individuals within the system must be viewed as agents for organizational learning. Argysis and Schon identify multichannel communications, networking, innovation, creativity, and risk taking as elements of a climate of learning.

A climate of learning, or a "learning culture," is much more than a policy of giving each worker so many days a year of training classes. It is an attitude and a management style, one that, like "total quality" or "service excellence," is a lot easier to give lip service than to execute successfully. It is important to realize that organizations with a focus on formal learning (training) alone do not necessarily provide climates of learning. Although learning goes on in training, it is primarily replicative learning. By contrast, a climate of learning is a radically different evolutionary process. It is not just an institution or organization full of people placing more emphasis on individual learning and spending more time at it. A learning climate is one where collaborative creativity in all contexts, relationships, and experiences is a basic purpose of the organization. It is a climate where the synergy, leadership, and the combined wisdom of groups is the measure of success. Rather than concentrating on individual learning, in a learning climate with multiple interactions among learning groups the whole unit learns in a self-aware, self-reflective, and creative way. The groups become the cells in the body of an organization, which, itself, becomes a new learning "individual" in the emergent global culture.

APPROACHES TO WPL
CLIMATE DEVELOPMENT

The importance of the environment for learning can not be overstated. Wolfe and Brandt (1998) state that

The brain changes physiologically as a result of experience. The environment in which a brain operates determines to a large degree the functioning ability of that brain. . . . The brain gobbles up the external environment through its sensory system and then reassembles the digested world in the form of trillions of connections which are constantly growing or dying, becoming stronger or weaker depending on the richness of the banquet. (p. 3)

Their study confirmed that the nervous system and the brain are the physical foundations of the human learning process. To promote learning, Wolfe and Brandt assert that the learning climate should be organized around real experiences and integrated, "whole" ideas, with a focus on learning that promotes complex thinking and the "growth" of the brain. Neuroscience proponents, like Wolfe and Brandt, advocate continued learning and intellectual development throughout adulthood.

Billington's (1998) study of learning environments and personal growth underscores this connection. She concluded, "results revealed that adults can and do experience significant personal growth throughout their lifetime. However, workers grew significantly only in the type of environment supportive of learning; they tended not to grow or to regress in other types" (p. 5). She was able to identify seven key factors in successful learning climates. These are the seven factors she found to be most important:

1. An environment where workers feel safe and supported, where individual needs and uniqueness are honored, where abilities and life achievements are acknowledged and respected;

2. An environment that fosters intellectual freedom and encourages experimentation and creativity;

3. An environment where supervisors treat workers as peers—accepted and respected as intelligent experienced adults whose opinions are listened to, honored, appreciated. Such supervisors often comment that they learn as

much from their employees as the workers learn from them;

4. Self-directed learning, where workers take responsibility for their own learning. They work with supervisors or HRD specialist to design individual learning programs which address what each person needs and wants to learn in order to function optimally in their profession;

5. Pacing, or intellectual challenge. Optimal pacing is challenging people just beyond their present level of ability. If challenged too far beyond, people give up. If challenged too little, they become bored and learn little;

6. Active involvement in learning, as opposed to passively listening to lectures. Where workers and supervisors or trainers interact and dialogue, where employees try out new ideas in the workplace, where exercises and experiences are used to bolster facts and theory, adults grow more; and

7. Regular feedback mechanisms for workers to tell managers what works best for them and what they want and need to learn—and supervisors who hear and make changes based on the input. (pp. 6-12)

One key element in promoting a workplace learning climate that is obvious from the above list is the leadership (supervision-management) of an organization. Nystrom (1990) presented a study that suggested leadership can impact organizational climate. According to his model, leadership can affect climate both directly and indirectly through impacting the direction and potential of the organization. Specifically, the higher the level of relationship between the leader and the follower, (i.e., the more support, trust, and autonomy), the more subordinates perceived the climate as supportive of workplace learning. This research suggests that leader behaviors that strengthen relationships with subordinates are associated with a stronger climate for learning. This model detailed below begins to explore the relationship between leadership behaviors and climate for learning.

- Fairness. The extent to which employees perceive their workplace to be equitable and free of bias.
- Safety. The extent to which employees perceive their workplace to be safe and free of physical danger.
- Support. The amount of perceived emotional support employees feel from the organization.
- Communication. The accuracy and openness of information exchange.
- Tolerance for Risk. The degree to which the organization encourages bold action, risk, and independence.
- Flexibility. The degree of adaptability and tolerance for ambiguity in an organization.
- Continuous learning. Perceptions of learning opportunities in the organization. (Nystrom, 1990, pp. 146-147)

Thus, according to Nystrom (1990), when a crisis hits, a company with a strong climate for learning might excel at turning the employee attention toward the developing problem in order to quickly generate solutions. Conversely, when an organization with a weak climate for workplace learning faces a crisis, it may take longer to focus employee attention toward finding potential solutions. In sum then, a strong climate for workplace learning aids in directing employee attention toward innovation. Leaders seeking to create innovation in their organizations, therefore, could potentially benefit from the establishment of a strong climate for learning. Given these findings, it would seem to benefit organizations to ensure that they create an environment that truly supports workplace learning.

Sambrook and Stewart (2000) feel that the correct approach to creating a learning climate at work is to persuade and encourage individuals that it is in their best interest to share what they know, and to learn from other people's experiences. According to them, "learning-enabled" organizational activities that encourage a "learning-aware" climate (and an environment conducive to knowledge exchange) should have a place for learner expression like a blog or similar device, have a place to connect the thoughts of other learners in a personal, meaningful way, have a place to dialogue with gurus (apprentice)—the heart of communities is the mesh of varying skills and expertise. Gurus are people currently in industry or established practitioners of the organizing theme of the community, and have a place for learning artifacts that are accessible and managed by the learner.

Finally, Marsick and Watkins (1993) suggest that organizations should 1) create continuous learning opportunities; 2) promote equity and dialogue; 3) encourage team learning and collaboration; 4) establish systems to capture and share learning; 5) empower people toward a collective vision; 6) support individuals in maintaining an openness toward new experiences, support in reflection, and support in translating the learning into practice; and, 7) connect the organization to its environment.

The most important conclusions to be drawn from these approaches to developing a learning climate is that attention must be paid to the processes within the organizations internal and external environment. Leaders can create opportunities for workplace learning by making space—physical and psychological—by modeling learning behaviors, and by rewarding learning. The challenge to those concerned with facilitating workplace learning is to become a human resource educator—one who draws out what is in other people. The challenge is to become a mentor of purpose and fulfillment for individuals, groups, and whole organizations.

CONCLUSION

Developing a supportive learning climate has emerged as a critical factor in workplace learning. Climate encompasses a range of ideas that suggest that various aspects of the internal work environment such as organizational culture, structure, leadership, policies, work practices regarding global issues, and a multinational workforce are likely to influence the learning of individuals, groups and the organization. External factors also influence the climate of the organization. Many organizations are looking for the best way to support workplace learning through the development of supportive learning climates.

Learning should be viewed as a systematic process. It needs to be fostered in each facet of an organization: in people and structures, in operational processes, in technological support, and in the various environmental concerns. Impediments to learning in any one of these areas can prevent individual and organizational learning. The learning environment is not a passive backdrop. It can distract or focus attention, impede or inspire learning, prevent or promote progress. The learning climate and culture can transform a static, passive state into a dynamic, active mental pursuit for knowledge. It can be the key to establishing a competitive advantage in any organization—large or small, for profit, non-profit, governmental, or NGO.

Therefore, the focus of organizations has turned to consideration of how to develop an appropriate learning climate, culture, environment, and set of processes that are linked to facilitating workplace learning. The recognition of the need for the organization to consider the organizational environment in its entirety to support Workplace Learning has gained importance. It has become clear that this extends further than merely providing learning opportunities at work. Watkins and Marsick (1993) for example state, "the creation of a learning environment goes far beyond the design of learning itself. It involves the design of work, work environments, technology, reward systems, structures, and policies" (p. 44). Determining those aspects of the organizational environment that support workplace learning is, therefore, critical in developing a comprehensive picture of those factors that constitute a continuous learning climate. This is becoming increasingly significant as the relationship between an organization's learning climate and a range of outcomes such as innovation, job performance, and organizational performance crystallizes.

CHAPTER 3
Individual Learning

Over the past few decades a shift in the understanding of how to best meet the needs of a well qualified and highly skilled workforce has occurred due to the major developments within the world of work. The reorientation back toward the workplace as the most effective means for developing employees has been one of the most significant changes (Conlon, 2004). This has given rise to the concept of workplace learning. Several key factors have driven this change. Workplace learning is seen as providing a continuum from formal education and training which prepares people for the world of work to lifelong learning strategy to achieve both social and economic goals in the area of competitiveness, flexibility, employability, and social inclusion (Billett, 2002). Research has identified this approach to employee development as offering considerable benefits over and above what has often been gained from formal training and education activities (Boud & Garrick, 1999; Toll, 1999). Traditional forms of employee development, such as deliberate, planned learning activities away from the work being performed, have not been adequate to meet many of the complex knowledge and skill needs required in today's workplaces (Fenwick, 2001; Norris, 2003).

Training has been criticized for focusing on rather narrow skill-based learning relevant for an employee to perform her or his current job, and that learning with a far greater application is needed for today's workplace (Boud & Garrick, 1999). In addition, formalized approaches to learning often are removed from the realities of the workplace, and suffer in terms of transferring learning to direct use on the job. It has also been criticized for often being seen to lack relevance to learners' needs (Bryans & Smith, 2000; Raelin, 2000). With the changes in the nature of the psychological contract between employers and employees the issue of relevance becomes even more important (Tennant, 1999). This means that by virtue of the unwritten employment contract they have with their employers, employees are increasingly demanding far more opportunities for career development and updating their skills in return for their labor and commitment to the organization. Organizations, especially those in high knowledge-intensive sectors or industries that wish to retain skilled employees, see offering continuing development opportunities as a key strategy for success (Conlon, 2004; Raelin, 2000).

The fact that workplace learning methods provide the most effective means for individuals to acquire the particular, and changing, types of skills and knowledge to operate effectively is beginning to be recognized by managers. Their task now is to consider how such learning can most effectively be supported and developed (Boud & Garrick, 1999; Bryans & Smith, 2000; Watkins & Marsick, 1993). Therefore, the concept of workplace learning breaks down the artificially created barriers between training and learning and work. As Raelin (2000) suggests,

> if knowledge is viewed as arising as much from active participation in the very apparatus of our everyday life and work, then we have to expand our conventional format of the classroom, and, indeed, interpret the workplace as a suitable locus of learning. (p. 280)

In this respect, the recognition that much learning actually occurs through self-directed mechanisms utilized by employees during the course of their work has extended previously held notions regarding the nature of learning itself.

However, the problem with many organizations is an over-emphasis on an outside-in, macro-organizational view of learning and an under-emphasis on the inside-out view which recognizes that people are the main agents of learning and change. Attempts at building an organization with a focus on workplace learning should start with an understanding of how adults learn and develop. Adult learning theory holds that people learn primarily by being encouraged to tackle challenges, experiment, fail and correct failures, and reflect on their experiences. A more thorough understanding of adult learning will enhance workplace learning.

ADULTS ARE NOT JUST BIG CHILDREN— AFTER ALL

As difficult as it is to believe, the massive and structured Training & Development efforts—as we know them now—only began in the latter part of the nineteenth century, just a little over 100 years ago, and did not really gain prominence until after World War II. The modus operandi of T&D was based on the only model of instruction available at the time: pedagogy (derived from "pede" meaning "child"). The only model anyone had was the school system, so training classes were organized along the lines and concepts of a school. Then, of course, *adults were taught as if they were children*. Instruction was essentially didactic. This means that the trainers are seen as the experts, the gurus, the masters, full of knowledge and wisdom. Their main job was to impart that knowledge and wisdom to the trainees. And, the participants were just empty vessels into whom the knowledge and wisdom were to be poured. This conjures up the image of class after class in buildings where adults were seated in rows and rows of desks and lectured to for long and boring hours.

Whether or not this is the best model for teaching children, it is clearly inadequate for adults—particularly when it comes to work or career-related learning. Adults desire a more active approach which takes into account individual experience. According to Merriam & Cafarella (1999), other researchers in the field of adult learning discovered that:

- in learning, adults don't behave as grown-up children
- adults learn best when they are consulted and actively

involved in determining what, how, and when they learn.

From these concepts a new teaching model began to emerge: andragogy ("andro" meaning "adult") as an alternative to pedagogy. A landmark book by Knowles (1970) solidified andragogy as being synonymous with adult learning. Knowles used andragogy to define and explain the conditions that adults require for learning. Initially defined as "the art and science of helping adults learn," the term has taken on a wider meaning and now refers to learner-focus education for people of all ages. For Knowles, andragogy is process-based rather than con-tent-(or product) based and anchored on four main assumptions (Knowles, 1980, pp. 44-45) about the characteristics of adult learners which, arguably, made them different from child learn-ers. Knowles later added a fifth assumption (Knowles, 1980, pp. 44-45), and then a sixth (Knowles, 1989, pp. 83-85). But even Knowles agrees that the first four, at least, differ only in degree between adults and children. The assumptions of andragogy did much to articulate how adults can be highly ef-fective and efficient learners if the following six specific con-cerns are addressed. The assumptions about adults are:

(1) Adults have a deep need to be <u>self-directing</u>
Adults have a strong self-concept of wanting to be in charge of their lives. They want to make decisions that will affect the quality of their lives. They don't readily accept the decisions of others.
(2) Adults have more and varied <u>experience</u> than youth
Unlike a child, adults have many years of experience. Adults' experiences make them the persons that they are. These experiences have been valuable in making who they are, and they want their experience to verify and validate the new learning. In other words, the more the new learning makes sense of their experiences, the more acceptable and durable the new learning will be. It's their way of making sense of the world they live in.
(3) Adults become <u>ready to learn</u> when they experience in

their life situation a need to know or be able to do in order to perform more effectively and satisfyingly.

It contrasts sharply to the pedagogy model which assumes that people are ready to learn when some authority figure (the teacher, the boss, etc) decides that they should; that they have to learn a topic or a subject simply because it is deemed good for them. On the other hand, adults learn best when they can see how the skill will help them in their lives and in their work, and they voluntarily choose to learn. To be forced to learn will only create resentment and resistance to acquisition of the new skills.

(4) Adults enter into a learning experience with a task-centered, (or problem-centered or life-centered) <u>orientation to learning</u>.

When adults enter the training room they will be asking questions such as: how will this new skill help them to solve their immediate problems, and how will it enhance the quality of their life. From these questions, it's obvious that adults are looking for the applicability and relevance of the training to their problems, their tasks and ultimately their lives. Children, in contrast, have a subject-centred orientation to learning. Their foremost thought is: I really want to learn this subject so that I will get good grades. Certainly, good grades matter, but to a child learning is all about grades. To a child, applicability and relevance of what they learn to their life is a secondary issue, not so adults.

(5) Adults are motivated to learn by both <u>extrinsic</u> and <u>intrinsic motivators</u>

The pedagogy model assumes that children are motivated to learn by extrinsic factors (good grades, parental approval, a new toy, getting that diploma or degree). Learning a subject just for the sheer joy of it seems a strange concept. To be sure, adults are also somewhat motivated by extrinsic factors (wage increase, recognition, promotion, etc). But the most potent motivators are intrinsic (self-esteem, growth, broader responsibilities,

power, achievements, and so forth).
(6) Adults have a need to know <u>why</u> they should learn
    something
    With the responsibility in earning a living and raising
    a family, many things demand the attention of adults.
    Before embarking on any field of study, they will want
    to know: what is in it for them, what do they really stand
    to lose if they don't learn this particular skill, and they
    need to be convinced (definitely much more than a
    child) that the time and effort learning the new skill is
    worth the sacrifice.

Employees of organizations are adult learners, and they
bring to their workplace an established body of knowledge,
skills, and certain abilities. Adult learners need to relate new
learning to their careers and experiences; they need to evaluate
new idea contexts as well. They also need support both from
within the organization and from outside the organization, and
they need a sense of control. They learn best by being helped
to create a sense of ownership of their learning. The work by
Knowles (1970, 1980, 1984), Merriam and Caffarella (1999),
Knowles, Holton, and Swanson (1998), and Brookfield (1986)
has also provided the basis upon which to compare the elements of the learning situation form a pedagogical and
andragogical perspective, as in Table 1 below.

To aid and promote workplace learners, the leaders in
organizations (especially HRD) should be familiar with why and
how adults learn and change. This knowledge of adult learning
can be used to promote effective learning activities. Organizations will need to set out to create an environment where employees can more easily learn what they need, when they need
it, and apply that knowledge, understanding and experience for
their own benefit as well as the organization's. To foster an
adaptive learning climate, workplace learning must offer employees two critical elements: proximity (which defines the
ease of access and level of integration provided to learning
resources) and relevancy (which defines the likelihood that what
is provided addresses the immediate learning needs of the indi-

Table 1. Comparison of Andragogy and Pedagogy

ELEMENTS	PEDAGOGICAL Teacher-Directed Learning	ANDRAGOGICAL Self-Directed Learning
Climate	Formal authority-oriented, Competitive Judgmental	Informal, mutually respectful, Consensual, Collaborative Supportive
Planning	Primarily by teacher	By participative decision making
Diagnosis of Needs	Primarily by teacher	By mutual assessment
Setting Goals	Primarily by teacher	By mutual negotiation
Designing a Learning Plan	Content units, Course syllabus, Logical sequence	Learning projects, Learning content sequences in term of readiness
Learning Activities	Transmittal techniques, Assigned readings	Inquiry projects, Independent study, Experimental techniques
Evaluation	Primarily by teacher	By mutual assessment of self-collected evidence

Developed from Knowles, 1970, 1980 & 1984

viduals who require workflow-based context for that experience). Relevancy requires context which adds a new dimension by providing an understanding of the individual performing the work. Learning environments that consider relevancy, context, and proximity will enable the learner to be more effective on the job. The learner will have the ability to choose when to learn, what to learn, and how to learn in environments that are not always formalized or traditional. In effect, become more self-directed.

SELF-DIRECTED LEARNING

One of the assumptions about learners that Knowles (1980) made was that they become increasingly self-directed as they mature. He viewed self-directed learning as a process where the individual took the primary responsibility for planning and carrying out his or her learning activities. Knowles (1975) defines self-direct learning as

> a process in which individuals take the initiative, with or without the help of others, in diagnosing their learning needs, formulating learning goals, identifying human and material resources for learning, choosing, and implementing appropriate learning strategies, and evaluating learning outcomes. (p. 18)

Similarly, Tough conducted some of the first comprehensive work in the field. Tough found that 70 percent of all learning activities were planned by the learners themselves (Tough, 1971). After these initial studies, others followed that debated what the goals of self-directed learning should be (Brookfield, 1986; Mezirow, 1985) and what the personal characteristics of self-directed learners were (Candy, 1991). One of the goals of self-directed learning was that it should foster transformational learning. This concept was mainly the work of Mezirow (1985) and Brookfield (1986). Mezirow suggested that self-knowledge was a prerequisite for autonomy in self-directed learning. Brookfield echoed Mezirow's ideas by asserting that "the most complete form of self-directed learning occurs when process and reflection are married in the adult's pursuit of meaning" (Brookfield, 1986, p. 38).

Even with the view of the varying purposes of self-directed learning, it is generally seen as self-learning in which the learners carry the primary responsibility for their learning. Self-directed learning occurs both inside and outside the formal learning environment, but does not mean that the learning occurs in isolation. In fact, self-directed learners often draw on the help of others as learning resources (Ellinger, 2004).

What these studies and their varying perspectives all agree on is that adults learn what they want to learn—what they value. Other things, even if acquired temporarily (i.e., for a test), are soon forgotten (Specht & Sandlin, 1991, as cited in Knowles,

Holton & Swanson, 1998). Employees may act as if they care about learning something, go through the motions, but then proceed to disregard it or forget it—unless, it is something which they want to learn. Even in situations where a person is under threat or coercion, a behavioral change displayed will typically extinguish or revert to its original form once the threat is removed (Raelin, 2000). This does not include changes induced, willingly or not, by chemical or hormonal changes in one's body. But even in such situations, the interpretation of the behavioral changes following it will be affected by the person's will, values, and motivations. Apparently, most if not all, sustainable behavioral change is intentional. From these studies, it appears that self-directed change is an intentional change in an aspect of who a person is, or who the person wants to be, or both. Self-directed learning is self-directed change in which the person is aware of the change and understands the process of change.

There are clear distinctions between self-directed people who drive their own development and careers and rise to new challenges through this change process, and the more traditional, passive learners who leave their career development to others. Self-directed learners generally hold an advantage over traditional approaches in the workplace, whether they are leaders, managers, or employees. Table 2 contains the characteristics of passive and self-directed learners. Self-directed learning can be more effective in worker development because learning

Table 2.

Passive learners. . .	Self-directed learners. . .
• Wanting others to give good feedback • Waiting for training • Waiting for their manager, mentor, or HR to structure their development • Expecting to be coached or managed • Expecting structured career paths	• Initiating feedback, and asking questions to extract maximum learning • Creating opportunities, structuring their own learning, volunteering • Seeking people they can learn from, and building networks of good relationships • Taking action to drive their career

accommodates employees' learning styles and objectives. It can save substantial training costs because learners learn to help themselves and each other with practical and timely materials, and it can achieve increased employee effectiveness in their jobs as they learn to learn from their own work experiences and actually apply their learning to their work.

Given, then, that self-directed learning is an important tool for workplace learning, the next concern is to discover ways that supervisors can help employees enhance self-directed learning in the workplace. The development of employees is impacted tremendously by the supervisor's attitude and knowledge about learning. Fisher (1995) gives numerous suggestions in order to better enable self-directed learning in the workplace. Some of the ways for supervisors and learners to turn the workplace into a learning laboratory are listed below:

1. Help the worker identify a starting point for a learning project and discern relevant ways of examination and reporting;

2. Encourage the learners to view knowledge and truth as contextual . . . and that they can act on their world individually or collectively to transform it;

3. Create a partnership with the worker by creating a learning contract for goals, strategies, and evaluation criteria;

4. Be a manager of the learning experience rather than an information provider;

5. Teach inquiry skills, decision making, personal development, and self-evaluation of work;

6. Help learners develop positive attitudes and feelings of independence relative to learning;

7. Recognize learners' personality types and learning styles;

8. Use techniques such as field experience and problem solving that take advantage of adults' rich experience base;

9. Encourage critical thinking skills by incorporating . . . such activities in seminars;

10. Create an atmosphere of openness and trust to promote better performance;

11. Behave ethically, which includes not recommending a self-directed learning approach if it is not congruent with the learners' needs;

12. Obtain the necessary tools to assess the learners' current performance, and to evaluate their expected performance;

13. Provide opportunities for self-directed learners to reflect on what they are learning;

14. Promote learning networks, study circles, and learning exchanges (self-managed teams of self-directed learners); and

15. Provide staff training on self-directed learning and broaden the opportunities for its implementation. (pp. 4-5)

Fisher adds that "self-directed learning is more than a form of education. It is a component in human development" (p. 7). But, only one component. By definition, self-directed learning requires that the learner think about and plan his or her learning. At times, learning in the workplace happens by accident, or in casual or informal settings. Informal learning (including incidental learning) is an important way for learning, as previously discussed in Chapter 1. Informal learning is related to, but not synonymous with, self-directed learning.

INFORMAL LEARNING

Informal learning flies under the radar screen. It can happen intentionally or by accident. No one takes attendance, for there are no classes. No one assigns grades, for success in life and work is the measure of its effectiveness. No one graduates, because learning never ends. Examples are learning through observing, trial-and-error, asking a coworker, traveling to a new place, reading a professional journal, conversing with others, taking part in a community, composing a story, reflecting on the day's events, awakening with an inspiration, raising a child, visiting a museum, pursuing a hobby, and on and on and on. Informal learning is based in conversations, social interactions, and team projects, in which learning is part of the interactions between people. It has been acknowledged as one of the key reasons for forming communities of practice, networks, and other forums that allow people to network and socialize. Informal learning is not limited to a predefined body of knowledge, but rather emerges from the interaction of people. At the heart of it is the transfer of tacit knowledge—knowledge that's not articulated but is acquired by individuals through experience.

Once again, Knowles is acknowledged for his pioneering work in the 1950s for informal adult education (Cseh, Marsick, & Watkins, 1999). Since then many authors have written about informal learning and offered their unique perspectives on the term. As noted earlier, Watkins and Marsick (1992) have identified the different forms of workplace learning as formal, informal, and incidental. Rusaw (1995) suggests that informal learning "is a process of learning that takes place in everyday experience, often at subconscious levels" (p. 218). Marsick and Watkins (1997) add that, not only is informal learning unique to the individual, but control of learning rests primarily in the hands of the learner. Stamps (1998, p. 32) asserts that informal learning is that "in which the learning process is neither determined nor designed by the organization, regardless of the formality or informality of the goals and objectives toward which the learning is directed."

Informal learning can also include unlearning old behaviors or practices that have negative consequences, or free people to make change (Cseh, Marsick, & Watkins, 1999; Rusaw, 1995). Informal learning strategies can also involve mentoring, coaching, networking, modeling, effective leadership and facilitation, interrelational aspects of teams, and individual characteristics and capabilities (Marsick & Watkins, 1990). In addition, employees can use informal learning to obtain help, information or support, learn from alternative viewpoints, gain ability to give greater feedback, consider alternative ways to think and behave (planned or unplanned), reflect on processes to assess learning experience outcomes, and make choices on where to focus their attention.

However, no one is suggesting that informal learning should be a replacement for formal activities; rather, it complements formal learning. Bell (1977) uses a metaphor of brick and mortar to describe the relationship between formal and informal learning in an organization. He explains that formal learning acts as bricks fused into the emerging bridge of personal growth. Informal learning serves as the mortar, facilitating the acceptance and development of formal learning. He feels that it is this synergy that produces effective growth in people. Thus, the two elements support one another, and neither would be effective without the other.

But, just as its important not to overlook the "mortar" in a structure, it is important not to overlook informal learning. Since studies have found that 70 to 80 percent of the learning that occurs is informal (Center for Workforce Development, 1998; Marsick & Watkins, 1990; Sorohan, 1993), it is important for organizations to foster informal learning. Informal learning can be encouraged and supported in the workplace without being forced on employees. A conscious decision can be made that formalized structured training may not be necessary except for the most technical or legal aspects. A new sales representative for a large multinational firm will likely need formalized training in the product line to be sold and to learn company and legal policies. However, training in workplace attitudes or specific, minute details of the job may hinder productivity, add costs, and seldom be used. The new sales representative will figure out what works best in practice. This may come from talking with individual customers, peer sales representatives, or simply perfecting a routine where better practices emerge through learned experience. Informal learning is voluntary and self-directed. It results from personal exploration and discourse and may occur spontaneously in everyday life situations, within the family circle, the neighborhood, and so on. The learner is motivated intrinsically (Cesh, Marsick, & Watkins, 1999) and determines the path to take to acquire the desired knowledge, skill, or abilities. The challenge for organizations, then, is to find the best way to facilitate self-directed and informal learning for its adult workers.

FACILITATING INDIVIDUAL LEARNING

The benefits of treating workers like the adult learners they are, allowing self-direction in deciding what, when, and how to learn, and valuing informal learning as highly as formal forms are best described in terms of the type of learners it develops. Adult learners, who are self-directed, demonstrate a greater awareness of their responsibility in making learning meaningful and monitoring themselves (Garrison, 1997). They are curious and willing to try new things, view problems as challenges, desire change, and enjoy learning (Taylor, 1995). Taylor also found them to be motivated and persistent, independent, self-disciplined, self-confident, and goal oriented.

Since these all seem to be desirable qualities in workers, the big question then is how organizations can promote self-directed, individual learning and also recognize informal learning opportunities. Garrison (1997) and Taylor (1995) stress that organizations that want to encourage learning need to free themselves from a preoccupation with tracking and correcting error, a practice that is ego-threatening to adults. Turning workers loose to decide what and how to learn, and what connections to make is a new concept in many organizations. Formal training programs often start with the mindset that learners are deficient, and the objective is to bring them up to par. Workers resent these assumptions. Their goals are to be the best that they can be, not just to get by. Optimism works better than pessimism.

Better to begin from positive assumptions, until proven wrong, than to let negativity eliminate options before they have been tested.

Most training looks at people as though they were missing something. The consequences of assuming the role of training is to fix what is broken rather than make what is already good better can be enormous and disastrous, such as:

- Largely ineffective negative reinforcement (correct what's wrong, take the test, do this or else) instead of the positive;
- Unmotivated learners (who wants to accept that they are inadequate?);
- Learner disengagement, unrewarded curiosity, spurned creativity (Because management implies "My way or the highway."); and
- Training (we do it to you) instead of learning (co-creation of knowledge);
- Disregard for creating new knowledge (for the trainer "knows it all") from the learning; (Fisher, 1995, p. 6)

Exchanging the concept of learning-as-medicine to cure deficiencies for the view of learning-as-growth experience is not something accomplished overnight. Shifts in organizational values and culture require a change-management approach that takes time. Garrison (1997) and Fisher (1995) advocate greater tolerance for uncertainty and encourage risk-taking, and capitalizing on learners' strong points instead of concontrating on weaknesses, as what workers perceive as beneficial to learn is likely to benefit the organization also.

There are several other suggestions to help organizations facilitate all forms of adult-focused, self-directed learning:

1. progressively decrease the workers' dependency on the trainer;

2. help workers to understand how to use learning resources—especially their experiences and the experiences

of others, including trainers, and how to engage others in reciprocal learning relations;

3. assist the worker to define his or her learning needs—both in terms of immediate awareness of understanding the culture, and psychological assumptions influencing her or his perceptions of needs;

4. assist workers to assume increasing responsibility for defining their learning objectives, planning their own learning programs, and evaluating their progress;

5. help workers identify strategies and resources to carry out their learning plan;

6. organize what is to be learned in relationship to his or her current personal problems, concerns, and levels of understanding;

7. provide opportunities for workers to apply their knowledge to work, family, and community settings;

8. foster worker decision making—facilitate taking the perspective of others who have alternative ways of understanding;

9. encourage the use of criteria for judging learning which are increasingly inclusive and differentiating in awareness, self-reflective, and integrative of experience;

10. facilitate problem posing and problem solving, including problems associated with the implementation of individual and collective action;

11. reinforce the self-concept of the worker by providing for progressive mastery, supportive climate with feedback to encourage efforts to change and to take risk; and,

12. emphasize experiential participative instructional methods, and appropriate use of modeling and learning contracts.

Making a concerted effort to provide the most effective means for individuals to acquire the particular and changing types of skills and knowledge to operate effectively will help ensure organizational success, and help promote meaningful learning for the adult worker.

CONCLUSION

When helping adults learn in the workplace, it is important to take into account some generally agreed upon characteristics of adult learners. Adults tend to be voluntary learners when given the option. They can direct their own learning by participating in its planning from the beginning stages. Adult learners are diverse and have a wealth of work experiences and well-developed personal identities which, when respected, provide a wonderful resource for the learning process. They make a voluntary commitment to learn when they experience a real need to know or to be able to do something. For many employees, the changing workplace has created this need.

Adults need to know why they are learning something. Learning is more effective when they understand how new knowledge will be immediately useful to them in their work or personal lives. Adults have clear learning objectives and need to know, through ongoing feedback, the extent to which their learning objectives are being met. There must be clear means and ends to their learning. They also have a high degree of motivation to learn. They respond to extrinsic motivators like high wages and promotion in the short term, but in the long term, intrinsic motivation like the need for self-esteem, recognition, and achievement fuel their passion. Their sense of self influences the learning situation in which they participate. Learning at work provides employees with the opportunity to participate with co-workers. This helps to diminish the fears held over from past school experiences and negative impressions of their own abilities, and places learning in an atmosphere in which they are already valued. This increased sense of *self* allows them to take control of their own learning and set the *direction* they decide.

Self-directed learning involves the worker taking the initiative to identify her or his learning needs and goals, and then selecting and using the learning strategies that work best for those needs. They can do this with or without the help of others in the organization. Unlike traditional training classes, with self-directed learning the workers are responsible for developing the learning skills, and deciding when and how they are going to learn. The benefits of self-directed learning include having greater control over learning and increasing their self-concept, motivation, and sense of self-control. Of course, self-directed learning increases the likelihood that informal learning opportunities will be enhanced.

Informal learning components stem from a variety of organizational work experiences, open-ended assignments, modeling of others' critical reflective learning, encouragement of questioning, honest feedback, participation in policy making and implementation, intercultural experiences in life, accepting another's help, information gathering, experimenting, listening to intuition, and examining issues from multiple perspectives. Informal learning can aid team building, and team members can be empowered by recognizing and using informal learning strategies. In addition, work context learning often occurs in unplanned ways, is tacit, non-linear and serendipitous as organizational participants are preoccupied with interpreting and understanding the changed environment. Reflection is a critical component of informal learning and is less of an outcome than on ongoing learning process. Informal learning can be facilitated by helping establish or allowing supportive mentoring relationships to flourish, encouraging communities of practice to dialogue informally on work-related issues of concern, providing skill development in process and facilitation to support reflective practice, and developing a shared set of values which reinforce the organization's commitment to learning.

CHAPTER 4
Social and Group Dimensions of Workplace Learning

Workers can no longer learn to operate one piece of equipment in their youth and continue to use that same skill for the next 40 years. Today, workers may need to learn to operate a new machine, or a new software program, or a new hardware configuration every 18 months or less (DeSimone, Werner, & Harris, 2002). When technology makes those old skills obsolete, workers may need to embark on a new career. The need to learn is accelerated by this environment of change. Learning has become part of the job for workers in virtually any organization, in any part of the world. And, while learning basic tasks is still a requirement for any situation, today's workers are also expected to master a higher order of learning—one that depends on interaction and collaboration with other workers (DeSimone, Werner, & Harris, 2002).

Employees are expected to work in self-directed teams to diagnose and solve problems. Workers use collaborative work groups to leverage each other's knowledge to gain a competitive advantage. They use research laboratories to build on the work of others to seek new solutions. If today's knowledge workers are to keep up with the world of change and the demands of collaborative work, the workplace will need to transcend its traditional role. It will have to be designed to provide more than just a site for activities, a shelter from the elements, or a place to listen to an "expert" disseminate information. It will have to function at a higher level that actively supports the kind of work and learning that takes place there.

FROM INDIVIDUAL TO COLLECTIVE LEARNING

Learning is a conscious attempt on the part of organizations to improve performance, effectiveness and innovativeness in uncertain economic and technological market conditions. The greater the uncertainties, the greater the need for learning. The importance of learning in an organization is not new. Learning enables quicker and more effective responses to a complex and dynamic environment. In turn, effective learning is associated with increased information sharing, communication, and understanding.

Traditionally, learning has been thought of as a solitary endeavor. In the past, the concept of learning in the organization was largely associated with individual learning in well-defined settings and under the domain of education and training. Individuals acquired knowledge and skills so that they could perform in their jobs. For example, in a keyboarding class for computer training at a social service agency, trainees may be given a drill to practice. A motivated learner may repeat the drill 10 times, training the mind and the hands to execute the keystrokes. A less-motivated learner may repeat the drill 3 times, achieving a lower level of learning. All workers are learning individually even though they are being taught in a group. The level of learning is not dependent upon interactions between the learners. Individual learning can take many forms from developing basic computer skills to memorizing advanced product information to acquiring the thinking skills required to solve complex problems.

Learning at the individual level can be accomplished to meet a range of needs from the most basic operating requirements to the most sophisticated demands for concept exploration and development. At the basic level, workers learn the rules of the workplace, the processes and procedures of the job, and the standards of safety and quality. This learning lays the groundwork for more advanced learning. At a more sophisticated level, the worker may learn to integrate the knowledge learned from other sources like supervisors and coworkers, or from experience on the job with their own thinking, analysis, and insights.

Passive approaches to learning assume that people "learn" by receiving and assimilating knowledge individually, independent from others (Bryans & Smith, 2000). In contrast, active approaches present learning as a social process which takes place through communication with others. The learner actively constructs knowledge by formulating ideas into words, and these ideas are built upon through reactions and responses of others (Bryans & Smith, 2000; Seely-Brown & Duguid, 2001). In other words, learning is not only active but also interactive.

In particular, collaborative or group learning refers to methods that encourage employees to work together on learning-type tasks. There was a time that if people "collaborated" while learning it was considered cheating. But now, the value of, in fact the need for, collaboration among workers is realized. Collaborative learning is fundamentally different from the traditional "direct-transfer" or "one-way knowledge transmission" model in which the instructor is the only source of knowledge or skills (Fenwick, 2001). In collaborative learning, instruction is learner-centered rather than teacher-centered, and knowledge is viewed as a social construct, facilitated by peer interaction, evaluation and cooperation. This conception of learning shifts the focus away from a "teacher-student" interaction to the role of peer relationships in learning success (Seely-Brown & Duguid, 2001). Therefore, the role of the trainer changes from transferring knowledge to trainees (the "sage on the stage") to being a facilitator in the learners' construction of their own knowledge (the "guide on the side").

Learning and development in the workplace is largely experience-based and social in nature (Bennis, 1997; Easterby-Smith, Snell & Geherdi, 1998; Raelin, 2000). The workplace provides countless learning opportunities in the form of new assignments and meaningful exchanges among peers. Experience gained from working through non-routine situations leads to modification of frames of reference and enrichment of the "repertoires of examples, images, understandings, and actions" ch workers draw in new situations (Schon, 1983, p. 138). ... e development of professional artistry through experience and reflection is an important aspect of workplace learning.

Collaboration is important at all levels and aspects of the organization. In a department, for example, workers may form teams to develop and test a new product. From discussion and sharing of ideas, each member of the group acquires a broad collection of perspectives and ideas, achieving higher understanding of alternatives and possibilities. The learning is dependent upon the interaction among the team members. No member of the group could achieve the same level of learning, and thus product knowledge, by reading material or doing independent development. Most believe learning is inherently a social process, yet in many organization environments, offices and workspaces are geared to individual work, thwarting collaborative efforts.

Social relationships within the work environment are an important source of learning in the workplace. As Jarvis (1987) asserts, learning in the workplace rarely happens "in splendid isolation" (p. 11). Learning involves more than cognitive processes. The socio-cultural environment affects what and how learning occurs and determines access to learning opportunities (Merriam & Cafarella, 1999). The social dimension of workplace learning also focuses on the dynamic relationship between an individual learner and his or her participation in teams or in a community of practice (Lave & Wenger, 1991; Wenger, 1998). The concepts of teamwork and communities of practice emphasize the socio-cultural conditions specific to the work environment and the situational nature of working and learning. The immersion of the whole person in the collective knowing process that can be characterized as interdependent and mutually shaping, moves the focus from the individual learner to the social dimension of learning.

TEAM LEARNING

A team, say Robbins and Finley, is "people doing something together. It could be a baseball team or a research team or a rescue team. It isn't what a team does that makes it a team; it is the fact that they do it together" (1995, p. 10). French and Bell (1995) feel that teams and teamwork are the driving force in organizations. A workplace team consists of "a number of persons, usually reporting to a common superior and having some face-to-face interaction, who have some degree of inter-dependence in carrying out tasks for the purpose of achieving organizational goals" (French & Bell, 1995, p. 169). They elaborate further by asserting that "a team is a small number of people with complementary skills who are committed to a common purpose, set of performance goals, and approach for which they hold themselves mutually accountable" (1995, p. 112).

Those who focus on the human side of organizations believe that individuals who have some control over how their work is done will be more satisfied and perform better. This is called empowerment. French and Bell (1995) assert that putting empowered individuals together into teams will yield extraordinary results:

> A fundamental belief . . . is that work teams are the build-ing blocks of organizations. A second fundamental belief is that teams must manage their culture, processes, systems, and relationships, if they are to be effective. Theory, research, and practice attest to the central role teams play in organizational success. (p. 87)

Senge (1990) considers the team to be a key learning unit in the organization. According to Senge, the definition of team learning is

> the process of aligning and developing the capacity of a team to create the results its members truly desire. It builds on the discipline of developing shared vision. It also builds on personal mastery, for talented teams are made up of talented individuals. (p. 236)

Senge (1990) describes a number of components of team learning. The primary component is dialogue. He identifies three conditions that are necessary for dialogue to occur: All participants must "suspend their assumptions"; all participants must "regard one another as colleagues;" and there must be a facilitator (at least until teams develop these skills) "who holds the context of the dialogue". He goes on to say that "hierarchy is antithetical to dialogue, and it is difficult to escape hierarchy in organizations" (p. 245). Suspending all assumptions is also difficult, but is necessary to reshape thinking about reality.

The goal of dialogue is to help the group bring assumptions to the surface and clarify theories-in-use, that is, what theoretical foundations they operate from. The first step must happen before a shared set of meanings and a common thinking process can be developed. This does not imply, however, that everyone must think alike. Groupthink—when people succumb to group pressure for conformity—is not a desirable condition. Group intelligence, where people reason and think collectively, is desirable (Senge, 1990).

According to West (1996), what begins as conversation is influenced by *crisis of suspension* and *crisis of collective pain*. People bring individual differences to the group, which can lead to conflict and defensive routines. When they engage in conversation, they share diverse ideas. This initiates a deliberation process and individuals decide at this point whether to suspend assumptions and move toward dialogue or beat down the opposing ideas. If the group can explore the differences and keep listening in order to learn, the crisis of suspension will be managed. The focus of the group then becomes collective inquiry, with new insights being developed. The crisis of collective pain refers to the challenge of accepting that isolation and fragmentation are created through one's own assumptions. As a group navigates this crisis, it begins to function as a whole, as opposed to working at cross-purposes, and a synergy develops. This alignment within groups is needed for team learning to occur. Thus, dialogue allows for the transformation of organizations, with members moving from individual, competing parts that are walled off from one another and reacting to external factors, to a collective, generative, boundary-crossing group.

But teams do not just happen. It takes time and effort to develop into high-performing teams where individual members trust each other and produce synergistic results. The process of team development is called team learning when the team consciously focuses on lessons learned over time. Facilitated reflection on team interactions and feedback on interpersonal behaviors and impact speed the process of team development (Norris, 2003).

Kasl, Marsick, and Dechant (1997, p. 238-40) have constructed a model of team learning which proposes four developmental stages to explain how team learning takes place in the workplace:

Phase 1: Fragmented Learning. Individual learning that is nei ther shared by a group nor necessarily shared with or by others.

Phase 2: Pooled Learning. Individuals share information and perspectives, and small groups of people learn together, but the group as a whole doesn't learn.

Phase 3: Synergistic Learning. Groups as a whole create knowledge mutually, integrating divergent perspectives in new ways but integrating team knowledge into individual meaning schemes.

Phase 4: Continuous Learning. Synergistic learning becomes habitual.

The authors emphasize that these phases are not linearly progressive steps, and groups can move back and forth among them.

Nador (2001) believes team learning can work but organizations need to make it happen. A good start is to identify organizational qualities and behaviors of team members that enhance team learning and help to create a learning culture. Nador's criteria for success in the promotion of team learning include these suggestions:

1. Team-oriented behaviors. Being a member of a team that

wants to learn as a group comes with certain responsibilities. Team members need to think not only about their own needs, but also the needs of others. Being part of an effective learning environment requires the following:

- Self-development: Every employee has a responsibility to read, attend conferences and do research to maintain a currency of knowledge and skills within their role. This includes sharing this knowledge when the employee leaves so that it is not lost.
- Knowledge-sharing: Every employee has a responsibility to be approachable, to answer questions of other team members and to have a keen desire to help others learn and succeed. This includes recognizing that team success can bring greater gains than individual success, and that offering information or resources, often unsolicited, will help others. An organization can integrate these behaviors into performance management and compensation programs.

2. Risk-oriented culture. Team learning is more successful when management is open to change, encourages innovation and supports the taking of risks within reasonable limits. It makes a big difference when a work environment encourages employees to challenge the status quo and involves them in changes that could benefit the organization.

3. Committed managers. Team learning can be a success if there are managers committed to the process who regularly schedule time to review work issues and challenges, past successes and failures. This means managers need to involve employees in the analysis of work problems to ensure they learn from their own experiences and those of others.

4. Recognition programs. Many organizations are introducing recognition programs, and those that have a commitment

to coaching, teaching and helping others can reinforce team values.

5. Team-based compensation. Similarly, compensation systems that recognize team efforts and success also reinforce organizational commitment to the team. (p. 2-3)

Once team learning has been successfully promoted, it is important to capture the group learning and make it a part of a knowledge repository that other employees can access easily. Boud and Garrick (1999) suggest reports, tours, cross-training, and personnel rotation plans as methods for transferring learning. If the learning of individuals is not transferred to the group or from the group to the organization, the learning will be lost. Institutional memory allows for new learning to build on past learning. Memory is not simply a storage device but an active component of learning as mental models shape how people act. Organizations with large turnover experience problems with learning because maintaining the shared models that allow for group learning becomes difficult. Teams need to share their learning across time and across vertical, horizontal, external, and geographic boundaries. By sharing learning across boundaries, it becomes less person-dependent and more embedded in the systems of the organization.

Senge (1990) believes that all knowledge is generated in working teams. He sees working and learning as inseparable. Through forming relationships, knowledge is diffused. He alludes to the image of the village square, where people hang out in a social space. That social space is the setting in which social relations are reinforced, trust is developed, and informal learning takes place. Informal learning is that which allows the tacit knowledge resident in a group to emerge and be exchanged, sometimes by serendipity, sometimes in the course of accomplishing a specific project, through the construction of spaces that support learning. In summary, team learning is the capacity of members of a team to suspend assumptions and enter into a genuine "thinking together." Team learning is vital because teams, not individuals, are the fundamental learning unit in modern organizations.

COMMUNITIES OF PRACTICE
IN THE WORKPLACE

In addition to believing that learning is something that individuals do, it is often assumed that learning has a beginning and an end, that it is best separated from other activities (such as work, for example), and that it is the result of teaching (Wenger 1998). However, contemporary thinking believes that learning is social and comes largely from the experience of participating in daily life. This rethinking of learning led Lave and Wenger (1991) to develop the notion of situated learning, that is learning involves a process of engagement in a *community of practice*. They assert that learning as it normally occurs is a function of the activity, context and culture in which it occurs or is situated. This contrasts with most formal learning activities which involve knowledge that is abstract and out of context. Social interaction is a critical component of situated learning—learners become involved in a community of practice which embodies certain beliefs and behaviors—the "practice" of the community. A community of practice (often given as CoP) is a network of people who share a common interest in a specific area of knowledge or competence, and are willing to work and learn together over a period of time to develop and share that knowledge. Everyone belongs to multiple communities of practice—family, civic groups, faith-based groups, professional associations, and so forth. Wenger (2002, p. 3) defines a community of practice as "groups of people who share a concern, a set of problems, or a passion about a topic, and who deepen their knowledge and expertise by interacting on an ongoing basis." He also believes that learning is a social activity, and that people learn best in groups.

Communities can vary quite widely in their characteristics. Some exist for years while others form around a specific purpose and disband once that purpose has been achieved. Members may be very similar (all engineers), or they may be multidisciplinary (engineers, accountants, marketing, etc), such as is often the case in communities that are formed around addressing a specific challenge. Some may be small and localized while others will be geographically dispersed "virtual communities" that communicate primarily by telephone, e-mail, online discussion groups or videoconferencing.

The idea of a community of practice has particular significance for organizations. The use of the apprenticeship model makes for a strong set of connections with important traditions of thinking about workplace learning within organizations. Perhaps more significantly, the growing interest in the learning organization has alerted organizations to the significance of informal networks and groupings. It has helped recognize communities of practice as valuable assets for organizations. The model provides a way of thinking about how benefits could accrue to the organization itself, and how value does not necessarily lie primarily with the individual members of a community of practice.

> Acknowledging that communities of practice affect performance is important in part because of their potential to overcome the inherent problems of a slow-moving traditional hierarchy in a fast-moving virtual economy. Communities also appear to be an effective way for organizations to handle unstructured problems and to share knowledge outside of the traditional structural boundaries. In addition, the community concept is acknowledged to be a means of developing and maintaining long-term organizational memory. These outcomes are an important, yet often unrecognized, supplement to the value that individual members of a community obtain in the form of enriched learning and higher motivation to apply what they learn. (Lesser & Storck, 2001, p. 837)

Lesser and Storck go on to argue that the social interaction resident in communities of practice leads to behavioral change—change that results in greater knowledge sharing, which in turn positively influences business performance. Attention to communities of practice could, thus enhance organizational effectiveness and profitability.

According to Wenger, a community of practice defines itself along three dimensions: what it is about—its joint enterprise as understood and continually renegotiated by its members; how it functions—mutual engagement that binds members together into a social entity; and, what capability it has produced—the shared repertoire of communal resources (routines, sensibilities, artifacts, vocabulary, styles, etc.) that members have developed over time (1998, pp. 73-84)

A community of practice involves much more than the technical knowledge or skill associated with undertaking some task. Members are involved in a set of longitudinal relationships (Lave and Wenger 1991) and communities develop around things that matter to people (Wenger 1998). The fact that they are organizing around some particular area of knowledge and activity gives members a sense of joint enterprise and identity. For a community of practice to function it needs to generate a shared repertoire of ideas, commitments and memories. It also needs to develop various resources such as tools, documents, routines, vocabulary and symbols that in some way carry the accumulated knowledge of the community. In other words, it involves practice: ways of doing and approaching things that are shared to some significant extent among members. The interactions involved, and the ability to undertake larger or more complex activities and projects though cooperation, bind people together and help to facilitate relationship and trust. Communities of practice can be seen as self-organizing systems, and they have many benefits.

Rather than looking to learning as the acquisition of certain forms of knowledge, Lave and Wenger have placed it in social relationships—situations of participation. As they put it, "rather than asking what kind of cognitive processes and conceptual structures are involved, ask what kinds of social engagements provide the proper context for learning to take place" (1991, p. 14). It is not so much that learners acquire structures or models to understand the world, but that they participate in frameworks that have structure. Learning involves participation in a community of practice. And that participation refers not just to local events of engagement in certain activities with certain people, but to a more encompassing process of being active participants in the practices of social communities and constructing identities in relation to these communities (Wenger, 2002).

Initially people who join communities learn at the periphery. As beginners or newcomers move from the periphery of this community to its center, they become more active and engaged within the culture and may eventually assume the role of expert or old-timer. As they become more competent they move more to the "center" of the particular community. Therefore, learning is not seen as the acquisition of knowledge by individuals so much as a process of social participation. The nature of the situation impacts significantly on the process. Learners inevitably participate in communities of practitioners and the mastery of knowledge and skill requires newcomers to move toward full participation in the socio-cultural practices of a community. "*Legitimate peripheral participation*" provides a way to speak about the relations between newcomers and old-timers, and about activities, identities, artifacts, and communities of knowledge and practice. It is legitimate because all parties accept the position of "unqualified" people as potential members of the community of practice. Peripheral because they hang around on the edge of the important stuff, do the peripheral jobs, and gradually get entrusted with more important tasks. Participation because it is through *doing* knowledge that they acquire it. Knowledge is situated within the practices of the community of practice, rather than something which exists "out there" in books. A person's intentions to learn are engaged, and the meaning of learning is configured, through the process of becoming a full participant in a socio-cultural practice. This social process includes the learning of knowledgeable skills. (Lave & Wenger, 1991, p. 29)

An example of this process would be when a new case worker comes to work for a social service agency. This new hire has worked in another agency and so brings some knowledge and experience with her to the new job. The first few weeks on the job she is on the periphery of the community watching, listening, and learning the norms of her new work setting. There are some old-timers here as well as others with various longevity on the job. She "practices" along with other community members and in this practice learns more about the work. As she becomes more knowledgeable she offers some of her previous experience to the group, thus contributing to the community through the work (the practice) of the group. Learning is spread across the community, and she gradually becomes a full participant in the community.

In this joining of community, there is a concern with identity, with learning to speak, act and improvise in ways that make sense in the community. What is more, and in contrast with learning as internalization, "learning as increasing participation in communities of practice concerns the whole person acting in the world" (Lave & Wenger, 1991, p. 49). The focus is on the ways in which learning is "an evolving, continuously renewed set of relations" (p. 50). In other words, this is a relational view of the person and learning. This way of approaching learning is something more than simply learning-by-doing or experiential learning. The concept of situatedness involves people being full participants in the world and in generating meaning. Lave and Wenger (1991, pp. 108-109) point out that "for newcomers the purpose is not to learn from talk as a substitute for legitimate peripheral participation; it is to learn to talk as a key to legitimate peripheral participation." This orientation has the definite advantage of drawing attention to the need to understand knowledge and learning in context.

Boud, Solomon, Leontios, and Staron (2001, pp. 37-38) assert that communities of practice are based on the following assumptions:

- *Learning is fundamentally a social phenomenon.* People organize their learning around the social communities to which they belong. Therefore, organizations are only powerful learning environments for workers whose social communities coincide with that organization.
- *Knowledge is integrated in the life of communities that share values, beliefs, languages, and ways of doing things.* Real knowledge is integrated in the doing, social relations, and

expertise of these communities.

- *The processes of learning and membership in a community of practice are inseparable.* Because learning is intertwined with community membership, it is what lets people belong to and adjust their status in the group. As they learn, their identity—and their relationship to the group—changes.
- *Knowledge is inseparable from practice.* It is not possible to know without doing. By doing, learning happens.
- *Empowerment—or the ability to contribute to a community—creates the potential for learning.* Circumstances in which people engage, in real action that has consequences for both them and their community, create the most powerful learning environments.

Communities of practice exist in some form in every organization—whether they have been deliberately created and labeled as such or not. The challenge for organizations is to support them in such a way that they make a positive contribution to creating and sharing organizational knowledge. Clemmons-Rumizen (2002) details some of the benefits of communities of practice as follows:

- Provide a valuable vehicle for developing, sharing and managing specialist knowledge
- Avoid "reinventing the wheel"
- Cut across departmental boundaries and formal reporting lines
- Can be more flexible than traditional organizational units Generate new knowledge in response to problems and opportunities
- Provide early warning of potential opportunities and threats
- Can be a vehicle for cultural change (creating a knowledge sharing culture)
- Are largely self-organizing. (p. 77)

As well as the organizational benefits, she contends that communities of practice also provide benefits for individual community members, including

Now what Obama is doing

- Having access to expert help to expand horizons, gain knowledge, and seek help in addressing work challenges
- Increasing member consciousness of, and confidence in, their own personal knowledge
- Providing a non-threatening forum to explore and test ideas, or validate courses of action
- Fostering a greater sense of professional commitment and enhance members' professional reputation.

There is a wide range of approaches to creating and developing communities of practice, and a wide range of resources full of guidelines and pointers. Since communities of practice are organic and self-organizing, ideally they should emerge naturally. Organizations that have tried to create communities "from the top down" have often failed. It is possible, however, that communities can be "seeded." Any area or function of an organization where knowledge is not evenly distributed is a potential target for a community of practice. However, the impetus for a new community usually comes from the recognition of a specific need or problem. Based on ideas put forth by Lave and Wenger (1991), Wenger (1998), Wenger (2002), and Clemmons-Rumizen (2002), the steps in fostering a community of practice will revolve around

1. **Defining the scope.** What is the domain of knowledge? At the heart of every community is a domain of knowledge; that domain can be either based around a professional discipline or on some specific problems or opportunities.

2. **Finding participants.** Who can make a major contribution to this community? Who are the subject experts, and possible coordinators, facilitators, and librarians and/or knowledge managers? Will membership be open or by invitation only?

3. **Identifying common needs and interests.** What are the core issues within the domain of knowledge? What are members interested in and passionate about? How do they

hope to benefit from membership of the community?

4. **Clarifying the purpose and terms of reference.** What are the specific needs or problems that should be addressed? What is the community setting out to achieve? How will the community benefit the organization? What are its values and ways of working? How will it be structured, organized and resourced?

It can often help to launch a community with a meeting or workshop so that members can meet each other and begin to develop relationships, and also spend some time together exploring and agreeing on their purpose, terms of reference, and ways of working. It is important to be sure that a community of practice is being promoted, not a team or work group.

Seely-Brown and Duguid (2001) believe that communities of practice differ from the usual notion of a team or work groups in a number of fundamental ways:

Voluntary membership. Where teams and workgroups are formed by management, membership in a community of practice is voluntary;

Specific focus. Teams and workgroups are formed to focus on a specific objective or activity, while communities of practice are not necessarily so focused; they may have some stated goals, but they are more general and fluid;

No expectation of tangible results. Teams and workgroups are required to deliver tangible results, whereas communities of practice are not necessarily;

Existence defined by group members. Teams and workgroups are disbanded or reorganized once they have achieved their goals, while communities of practice last as long as their members want them to last.

Wenger (2002) asserts the community of practice concept has been adopted most readily by people in business organizations because of the recognition that knowledge is a critical asset that needs to be managed strategically. Initial efforts at managing knowledge had targeted information systems with disappointing results. Communities of practice provided a new approach, which focused on people and on the social structures that enable them to learn with and from each other. Today, asserts Wenger, there is hardly any organization of a reasonable size that does not have some form of communities-of-practice initiative. A number of characteristics explain this rush of interest in communities of practice as a vehicle for developing strategic capabilities in organizations:

- Communities of practice enable practitioners to take collective responsibility for managing the knowledge they need, recognizing that, given the proper structure, they are in the best position to do this.
- Communities among practitioners create a direct link between learning and performance, because the same people participate in communities of practice and in teams and business units.
- Practitioners can address the tacit and dynamic aspects of knowledge creation and sharing, as well as the more explicit aspects.
- Communities are not limited by formal structures: they create connections among people across organizational and geographic boundaries. (pp. 141-143)

From this perspective, the knowledge of an organization lives in a constellation of communities of practice each taking care of a specific aspect of the competence that the organization needs. However, the very characteristics that make communities of practice a good fit for stewarding knowledge—autonomy, practitioner-orientation, informality, crossing boundaries—are also characteristics that make them a challenge for traditional hierarchical organizations.

Communities can naturally fade away and this is not always a bad thing. Sometimes a natural ending is reached when a group of people or a practice reaches a natural conclusion.

Other times a community can break up and in its place, a number of "subcommunities" based around particular specialist subject emerge. Either way, when a community fades it is important to celebrate its life and achievements, and to ensure that the relevant body of knowledge is captured and/or transferred.

CONCLUSION

The distinction between communities and teams sometimes leads to confusion. Storck and Hill (2000) suggest that the differences between the two constructs can be characterized as follows:

1. Team relationships are established when the organization assigns people to be team members. Community relationships are formed around practice.

2. Similarly, authority relationships within the team are organizationally determined. Authority relationships in a community of practice emerge through interaction around expertise.

3. Teams have goals, which are often established by people not on the team. Communities are only responsible to their members.

4. Teams rely on work and reporting processes that are organizationally defined. Communities develop their own processes.

Others tie the difference between teams and communities to the legitimizing process (Hackman, 1990; Norris, 2003; Rusaw, 1995). In a team, legitimizing occurs principally through the assignment of formal roles and relationships (i.e., team membership and structure are defined external to the team). Members of a community of practice establish their legitimacy through interaction about their practice.

Yet, teams have proven themselves to be more than just the latest "buzz word." Teams can accomplish more work and produce better results because of the vast amount of information available and the speed of change in the organizational environment. No one person can keep up with the explosion of information and constant change and still be productive.

The changing paradigm in the workplace has created an environment that emphasizes learning as the core activity of all types of organizations, whether profit, non-profit, government, or NGO. Collaborative learning should be the model of the future for organizations that champion generative learning over adaptive learning. If the desire is to produce knowledge able workers, then there will need to be a move toward rewarding cooperation and collaboration rather than competition between individuals. Alignment, shared mental models, and constant reflection on underlying assumptions will be major foci of group learning in the workplace. The world of work is changing and instead of learning particular jobs, people need to begin to learn about working under different conditions, in multiple roles, on multiple teams, and in multiple communities of practice.

CHAPTER 5
Organizational Learning

It is clear that continuous learning is playing an increasingly important role in today's organizations that are constantly challenged to perform beyond their current capabilities. Frequent changes in technology, globalization of services, and shifting customer demands require "smart" organizational strategies. Successful organizations will need to learn from experience and understand how to continually adapt to new conditions (DiBella & Nevis, 1998; Giesecke, 2004). Increasing demands of the workplace require modes of continuous learning, participatory management and worker involvement in decision-making, high performing self-directed work teams that require learning to manage projects, increased need for service orientation, and the ability to influence others (Watkins & Marsick, 1993). Thus, in order "to survive in the turbulent environment created by these forces, organizations and their workforces must be flexible, farsighted, and able to learn continuously (DeSimone, Werner, & Harris, 2002, p. 5).

The underlying cause for this recent emphasis on organizational learning is because of the increased pace of change. Classically, work has been thought of as being conservative and difficult to change. Learning was something divorced from work, and innovation was seen as the necessary but disruptive way to change. The organization that is able to quickly learn and then innovate its work will be able to change its work practices to perform better in the constantly changing environment. Change is now measured in terms of months not years as it was in the past. Organizations used to concentrate on eliminating waste rather than on working smarter and learning.

Organizational learning is a fairly recent way to think about learning in organizations. In a time of less organizational change (technological, societal, and economic) it was possible for an organization to develop a strategy for functioning, and assuming the strategy was initially effective, maintain that strategy for several decades. Current organizations, however, must change constantly in order to survive for even a portion of a decade. The competitive landscape is not changing in a linear, predictable manner, and the future cannot be assumed to be a simple extrapolation of the past (Rowden, 2001). But change, in and of itself, is not sufficient. The change must be based on appropriate data, gathered externally from the environment and internally from lessons learned. Both are a part of organizational learning and both are critical to effective organizations. The focus of organizational learning is on the processes through which the organization as a system learns, rather than the more typical focus on the learning that individuals within the organization accomplish.

The examination of organizational learning should not focus on static entities called organizations, but with the active process of organizing. Individual members are continually engaged in attempting to know the organization, and to know themselves in the context of the organization. At the same time, their continuing efforts to know and to test their knowledge represent the object of their inquiry. With the current flood of mergers and acquisitions, restructuring, globalization, and job outsourcing, some organizations provide a context for individuals and teams to negotiate effectively the kind of change which has become prevalent in today's workplace. A focus on organizational learning contributes to employees' collective ability to move beyond simply coping with change to engaging in creative action, for the benefit of both the individual members and the organization as a whole.

ORGNIZATIONAL LEARNING

The emergence of the idea of organizational learning is closely associated with ideas such as the learning society. Perhaps the most significant earlier contribution to the idea of the learning society was made by Schon (1973). He provided a theoretical framework linking the experience of living in a situation of increasing change with the need for learning:

> The loss of the stable state means that our society and all of its institutions are in continuous processes of transformation. We cannot expect new stable states that will endure for our own lifetimes . . . We must learn to understand, guide, influence and manage these transformations. We must make the capacity for undertaking them integral to ourselves and to our institutions . . . We must, in other words, become adept at learning. We must become able not only to transform our institutions, in response to changing situations and requirements; we must invent and develop institutions which are "learning systems," that is to say, systems capable of bringing about their own continuing transformation. (Schon, 1973, p. 28)

One of Schon's innovations was to explore the extent to which companies, social movements and governments were learning systems—and how those systems could be enhanced. He suggested that the movement toward learning systems is, of necessity, "a groping and inductive process for which there is no adequate theoretical basis" (1973, p. 57). The organization, Schon argued, was a striking example of a learning system. He makes the case that many organizations no longer have a stable base in the technologies of particular products or the systems built around them. Schon argued that "change" is a fundamental feature of modern life and that it is necessary to develop social systems that can learn and adapt. Early on Schon cultivated many of the themes that were to emerge later as a significant part of his collaboration with Argyris, and his exploration of reflective practice. Argyris and Schon (1978) then went on together to develop their seminal work that defined the concept of organizational learning.

Argyris and Schon (1996) suggest that each member of an organization constructs his or her own representation or image of the theory-in-use (theories that drive their actions) of the whole. A theory-in-use is the worldview and values implied by their behavior, or the maps they use to take action; whereas, espoused theory is the worldview people *believe* their behavior is based on. That is, people are unaware that their theories-in-use are often not the same as their espoused theories. The picture is always incomplete—and people, thus, are continually working to add pieces and to get a view of the whole. They need to know their place in the organization, Argyris and Schon argued. An organization is like an organism each of whose cells contains a particular, partial, changing image of itself in relation to the whole. And like such an organism, the organization's practice stems from those very images. With these sets of reflections, it becomes apparent how Argyris and Schon connect up the individual world of the worker and practitioner with the world of the organization.

Much of the more recent effort has been devoted to identifying templates, or ideal forms, which real organizations could attempt to emulate (Easterby-Smith & Araujo, 1999). The central template or ideal form typically has come to be the notion of the learning organization. As a result, the views on organizational learning have basically fallen into two camps: organizational learning as a technical process or a social process.

> The *technical* view assumes that organizational learning is about the effective processing, interpretation of, and response to, information both inside and outside the organization. This information may be quantitative or qualitative, but is generally explicit and in the public domain. . . . The *social perspective* on organization learning focuses on the way people make sense of their experiences at work. These experiences may derive from explicit sources such as financial information, or they may be derived from tacit sources, such as the "feel" that a skilled craftsperson has, or the intuition possessed by a skilled strategist. From this view, learning is something that can emerge from social interactions, normally in the natural work setting. In the case of explicit information it involves a joint process of making sense of data . . . The more tacit and "embodied"

forms of learning involve situated practices, observation and emulation of skilled practitioners and socialization into a community of practice. (Easterby-Smith & Araujo, 1999, pp. 3-5)

An example of the technical view is the work of Argyris and Schon on single- and double-loop learning, and deutero-learning (1978, 1996). In single-loop learning, individuals, groups or organizations modify their actions according to the difference between expected and obtained outcomes. In double-loop learning, the entities (individuals, groups or organization) question the values, assumptions and policies that led to the actions in the first place; if they are able to view and modify those, then double-loop learning has taken place. Double-loop learning is the learning about single-loop learning. With single-loop learning, people learn about what happened and change in response, but they do not uncover and examine underlying mental models. In double-loop learning, they examine why something happened, surfacing and examining the underlying mental models. Double-loop learning involves interrogating the governing variables themselves and often involves radical changes such as the wholesale revision of systems, alterations in strategy, and so on. This is particularly useful for solving complex problems that change over time.

Deutero-learning focuses on learning how to learn (Argyris & Schon, 1996). The members of an organization ask more and more fundamental questions about their organization, reflect on, and examine the previous contexts for leaning. Practitioners of workplace learning can encourage deutero-learning by helping workers identify their preferred learning styles, examine the effects of those learning styles, and learn effective strategies for enhancing their learning styles. Argyris and Schon write that this level of organizational learning refers to the organizational capacity to set and solve problems, and to design and redesign policies, structures, and techniques in the face of constantly changing assumptions about the organization and the environment. All three levels of learning can occur in organizational learning, but double-loop and deutero-learning are of critical importance to enhance the survival and success of organizations.

Ashton (2004) further explored Argyris and Schon's original perspective of organizational learning as a process of detecting and correcting error. Not error from the standpoint of doing something wrong or trial-and-error, but, in their view, error is any feature of knowledge or knowing that inhibits learning. In this way, single-loop learning can be compared to a thermostat that learns when it is too hot or too cold, and then turns the heat on or off. The thermostat is able to perform this task because it can receive information (the temperature of the room) and therefore takes corrective action. Of course, the thermostat never checks to see if a door or window has been left open. If the thermostat could question itself about whether it should be set at 70 degrees or if the window should be closed, it would be capable not only of detecting error but of questioning the underlying policies and goals. This second, more comprehensive inquiry, would be an example of double-loop learning. Another example of the concept would be when a plant managers and marketing people are detecting and attempting to correct error in order to manufacture Product X—single-loop learning. Confronting the question of whether Product X should be manufactured at all, would be an example of double-loop learning, because they are now questioning the organization's underlying policies and objectives.

As previously discussed in Chapter 4, Lave and Wenger (1991) and Wenger (1998) provide an example of the social perspective in their studies of communities of practice. Schon (1983) also provides some insights into the use of "tacit" sources (versus the technical perspective) in his exploration of reflective practice. Those operating within this social perspective may view organizational learning as a social construction, as a political process, and/or as a cultural artifact.

Perhaps the most recognizable and noted example of the social perspective is the concept of the learning organization as presented by Senge (1990). It is not a different form of organizational learning, but is merely a process or concept within organizational learning. Generally, a learning organization is viewed as one that learns and encourages learning among its people. It promotes exchange of information between workers hence creating a more knowledgeable workforce. This produces a very flexible organization where people will accept and adapt to new ideas and changes through a shared vision. Some specific definitions from the literature are:

> Learning organizations [are] organizations where people continually expand their capacity to create the results they truly desire, where new and expansive patterns of thinking are nurtured, where collective aspiration is set free, and where people are continually learning to see the whole together. (Senge, 1990, p. 3)

> The Learning Company is a vision of what might be possible. It is not brought about simply by training individuals; it can only happen as a result of learning at the whole organization level. A Learning Company is an organization that facilitates the learning of all its members and continuously transforms itself. (Pedler, Burgoyne, & Boydell, 1991, p. 1)

> Learning organizations are characterized by total employee involvement in a process of collaboratively conducted, collectively accountable change directed towards shared values or principles. (Watkins & Marsick 1993, p. 118)

The concept of the learning organization arises out of ideas long held by followers of collaborative learning. One of the specific contributions of the learning organization is its focus on the humanistic side of organizations. The learning organization perspectives "differ from more familiar management disciplines in that they are "personal" disciplines. Each [perspective] has to do with how we think, what we truly want, and how we interact and learn with one another" (Senge, 1990, p. 11). Currently, there are no known true learning organizations. However, some of today's most successful organizations like GE General Electric), Microsoft, and Southwest Airlines are embrac-

ing these ideas to meet the demands of a global economy where
the individual is increasingly recognized as the most important
resource.

Senge (1990; 1996) believes that those who work in a
learning organization are "fully awakened" people. They are
engaged in their work, striving to reach their potential, by sharing the vision of a worthy goal with team colleagues. They
have mental models to guide them in the pursuit of personal
mastery, and their personal goals are in alignment with the
mission of the organization. Working in a learning organization
is far from being a slave to a job that is unsatisfying; rather, it is
seeing work as part of a whole, a system where there are
interrelationships and processes that depend on each other.
Consequently, awakened workers take risks in order to learn,
and they understand how to seek enduring solutions to
problems instead of quick fixes. Lifelong commitment to high
quality work can result when teams work together to capitalize
on the synergy of the continuous group learning for optimal
performance. Those in learning organizations are not slaves to
living beings, but they can serve others in effective ways because they are well-prepared for change and working with
others.

Senge (1990) explains that there are five disciplines which
have to be mastered to have such an organization:

1. Systems Thinking—the ability to see the big picture, and
   to distinguish patterns instead of conceptualizing change
   as isolated events. Systems thinking needs the other four
   disciplines to enable a learning organization to come about.
   There has to be a paradigm shift from being unconnected
   to interconnected to the whole, and from blaming problems on something external, to a realization that how we
   operate, our actions, can create problems. (p. 10)

2. Personal Mastery—begins "by becoming committed to . . .
   lifelong learning," and is the spiritual cornerstone of a
   learning organization. Personal Mastery involves being more
   realistic, focusing on becoming the best person possible,

and to strive for a sense of commitment and excitement in our careers to facilitate realization of potential. (p. 11)

3. Mental Models—they must be managed because they do prevent new and powerful insights and organizational practices from becoming implemented. The process begins with self-reflection, unearthing deeply held belief structures and generalizations, and understand how they dramatically influence the way we operate in our own lives. Until there is realization and a focus on openness, real change can never be implemented. (p. 12)

4. Building Shared Visions—visions cannot be dictated because they begin with the personal visions of individual employees, who may not agree with the leader's vision. What is needed is a genuine vision that elicits commitment in good times and bad, and has the power to bind an organization together. As Senge contends, "building shared vision fosters a commitment to the long term" (p. 12)

5. Team Learning—is important because currently, modern organizations operate on the basis of teamwork, which means that organizations cannot learn if team members do not come together and learn. It is a process of developing the ability to create desired results; to have a goal in mind and work together to attain it. (p. 13)

According to Bennis (1997), "the most successful corporation . . . will be something called a learning organization, a consummately adaptive enterprise" (p. 11). But Senge (1996) argues that increasing adaptiveness is only the first stage in moving toward becoming a learning organization. The impulse to learn in children goes deeper than desires to respond and adapt more effectively to environmental change. The impulse to learn, at its heart, is an impulse to be generative, to expand capability. This is why leading corporations are focusing on generative learning, which is about creating, as well as adaptive learning, which is about coping. A learning organization does away with the mentality that it is only senior management that does all the thinking for the entire organization. It challenges all employees to tap into their inner resources and potential, in hopes they can build their own community based on principles of liberty, humanity, and a collective will to learn.

To tap into this inner resource and potential, organizations will continue to look for ways to improve workplace learning and deal with necessary change. As Garvin (1994) asserts, "continuous improvement requires a commitment to learning" (p. 19). Change is the only constant that should be expected in the workplace, and therefore, the organization needs to abandon the traditional, hierarchal structures that are often "change-averse," or undergo change only as a reaction to external events (West, 1994). Learning organizations embrace change and constantly create the reference points to precipitate an ever-evolving structure that has a vision of the future built-in.

According to Raelin, (2000), a learning organization is a healthier place to work because it

- promotes independent thought
- increases the ability to manage change
- improves quality
- develops a more committed work force
- gives people hope that things can get better
- stretches perceived limits
- is in touch with a fundamental part of a person's humanity — the need to learn, to improve the environment, and to be active actors, not passive recipients. (Raelin, 2000)

According to Senge (1996), effective leadership is the very first thing needed to create a learning organization. Not leadership based on traditional hierarchy, but a mix of different people from all levels of the system to lead in different ways. There also needs to be the realization that everyone has the inherent power to find solutions to the problems organizations face, and that everyone can and will envision a future for the organization and forge ahead to create it. As Gephart, Marsick, Van Buren, and Spiro (1996) point out, "the culture is the glue that holds an organization together; a learning organization's culture is based on openness and trust, where employees are supported and rewarded for learning and innovating, and one that promotes experimentation, risk taking, and values the well-being of all employees" (p. 39).

Overall, to create a culture and environment that will be the foundation for a learning organization, people need to realize the beginning comes with "a shift of mind—from seeing ourselves as separate from the world to connected to the world; from seeing ourselves as integral components in the workplace, rather than as separate and unimportant, robotic caricatures" (Senge, 1996, p. 37). Finally, identifying and breaking down the ways people reason defensively is one of the biggest challenges that has to be overcome in any organization. Until then, change can never be anything but a passing phase (Argyris, 1991).

Even when it is accepted that a learning organization is a desirable state for an organization, it can be difficult to understand how to achieve the principles of a learning organization. The first thing to do is to create a timeline to initiate the types of changes that are necessary to achieve the principles of a learning organization. The timeline, in order of appearance, might look something like the following:

- First, create a communications system "to facilitate the exchange of information, the basis on which any learning organization is built" (Gephart, et al., 1996, p. 40). The use of technology has and will continue to alter the workplace by enabling information to flow freely, and to "provide universal access to business and strategic information"(Gephart, et al., 1996, p. 41). It is also important in clarifying the more complex concepts into more precise language that is understandable across departments. (Kaplan & Norton, 1996)
- Second, organize a *readiness questionnaire*: a tool that assesses the distance between where an organization is and where it would like to be, in terms of the following seven dimensions. "Providing continuous learning, providing stra-

tegic leadership, promoting inquiry and dialogue, encouraging collaboration and team learning, creating embedded structures for capturing and sharing learning, empowering people toward a shared vision, and making systems connections" (Gephart, et al., 1996, p. 43). This questionnaire will be administered to all employees or a sample of them, and will develop an assessment profile, used to design the learning organization initiative. (Gephart, et al., 1996)

- Third, commit to developing, maintaining, and facilitating an atmosphere that promotes learning.
- Fourth, with the help of all employees, create a vision of the organization and write a mission statement. (Gephart, et al., 1996)
- Fifth, through workplace learning and awareness programs, try to expand employees' behaviors to develop skills and understanding needed to reach the goals of the mission statement, including the ability to work well with others, become more verbal, and network with people across all departments within the organization. (Easterby-Smith & Araujo, 1999)
- Sixth, "communicate a change in the company's culture by integrating human and technical systems" (Gephart, et al., 1996, p. 44).
- Seventh, initiate the new practices by emphasizing team learning and contributions because workers will become more interested in self-regulation and management, and be more prepared to meet the challenges of an ever-changing workplace. (Gephart, et al., 1996, p. 44)
- Eighth, allow employees to question key organizational practices and assumptions.
- Ninth, develop workable expectations for future actions. (West, 1994)
- Tenth, remember that becoming a learning organization is a long process and that small setbacks should be expected. It is the journey that is the most important thing because it brings everyone together to work as one large team. In addition, it has inherent financial benefits by turning the

workplace into a well-run and interesting place to work; a place which truly values its employees.

To be sure, although the concept of the learning organization is obviously related to organizational learning, they are not synonymous. It is easy to confuse the two, but organizational learning is a concept of its own. Schwandt and Marquardt (2000) believe that organizational learning is a process that may or may not result in a learning organization. They contend that organizational learning is a process whereas a learning organization is a product. A learning organization is a representation of a desired end. Organizational learning is the "dynamic human process required to increase the cognitive capacity of the total organization" (Schwandt & Marquardt, 2000, p. 28). A goal of organizational learning is to encourage individual learning at the team and group level. Organizational learning is a process through which organizations gain experience, reflect upon that experience, and anticipate new experience to help the organization perform at optimum ability. It means learning at the system level.

As a result of their work discussed earlier, Argyris and Schon (1978) were able to identify several ways to conceptualize organizational learning. Each perspective sheds light on organizational learning in a different way:

> First, the organization can be viewed as a group of people . . . Second, the organization can be regarded as a vehicle by which to achieve social objectives . . . Third, the organization can be regarded as a social structure . . . Fourth, the organization can be regarded as a system . . . Fifth, organizational learning can be viewed from the perspective of corporate culture. . .Sixth, organizations can be viewed as political systems in which individuals form groups and then attempt to gain advantage or power through deliberative group action. (p. 329)

Regardless of how organizational learning is conceptualized, learning is a conscious attempt on the part of organizations to retain and improve competitiveness, productivity, and innovativeness in uncertain technological and market circumstances. The greater the uncertainties, the greater the need for learning. Organizations learn in order to improve their adaptability and efficiency during times of change (Dodgson, 1993). Grantham and Nichols (2003) state that learning enables quicker and more effective responses to a complex and dynamic environment. Learning also increases information sharing, communication, understanding, and the quality of decisions made in organizations.

CAN ORGANIZATIONS LEARN?

However, one lingering question remains—Can organization truly learn? Although the subject of individual learning has been rather deeply researched for some time now, organizational learning, which draws on the integration of the sum of individuals' learning to create a whole that is greater than the sum of its parts, is far less understood (Grantham & Nichols, 2003). DiBella and Nevis (1998) believe that all organizations learn, whether they consciously chose to or not, because it is a fundamental requirement of their sustained existence. But they feel that organizational learning is both quantitatively and qualitatively distinct from the sum of the learning process of individuals. Stata (1999) describes several ways that organizational learning differs from individual learning:

> First, organizational learning occurs through shared insights, knowledge, and mental models. Thus organizations can learn only as fast as the slowest link learns. Change is blocked unless all of the major decision makers learn together, come to share beliefs and goals, and are committed to take the actions to change. Second, learning builds on past knowledge and experience—that is, on memory. Organizational memory depends on institutional mechanisms (e.g., policies, strategies, and explicit models) used to retain knowledge. Of course, organizations also depend on the memory of individuals. But relying exclusively on individuals risks losing hard-won lessons and

experiences as people migrate from one job to another. (p. 74)

Gephardt, et al., (1996) write that since organizations are not living organisms they do not learn the same way that individuals do, and that organizational learning is unique to an institution. Organizational learning takes place through the medium of individuals and their interactions, which together constitute a different whole, with its own capabilities and characteristics. Hedberg asserts,

> Although organizational learning occurs through individuals, it would be a mistake to conclude that organizational learning is nothing but the cumulative results of their members' learning. Organizations do not have brains, but they have cognitive systems and memories. As individuals develop their personalities, personal habits, and beliefs over time, organizations develop worldviews and ideologies. Members come and go, and leadership changes, but organizations' memories preserve certain behaviors, mental maps, norms, and values over time. (1991, p. 3)

Conversely, others, like Prange (1999) and Salomon, 1993), comment that one of the greatest mis-directions of organizational learning is the "who question," that is, "the way in which learning might be considered organizational" (Prange, 1999, p. 27). Some argue that it is individuals, not organizations, who learn. This view that learning is the sum of individuals refers to the processes of thinking and remembering that take place within an individual's brain. Traditionally, the study of cognitive processes, cognitive development, and the cultivation of desirable skills and competencies has treated everything cognitive "as being *possessed* and residing *in the heads* of individuals; social, cultural, and technological factors have been relegated to the role of backdrops or external sources of stimulation" (Salomon, 1993, p. xii)

However, people appear to think in conjunction or partnership with others and with the help of culturally provided tools. Cognitive processes do not seem to be content-free tools that are brought to bear on this or that problem. Instead, cognition will emerge in a situation tackled by teams of people and with the tools available to them. It is not just the "person-solo" who learns, but the "person-plus," the whole system of interrelated factors. (Salomon, 1993, p. xiii)

In summary, organizations, like individuals, can learn. Many of the fundamental phenomena of learning are the same for organizations. However, organizational learning also has distinctive characteristics with reference to what is learned, how it is learned, and the adjustments called for to enhance learning. These derive from the fact that any organization by definition is a collective, with individuals and larger units in different roles that involve different perspectives and values, passing information through their own filters, and with noisy and loss-prone information channels connecting them. In the final analysis, the only resource capable of learning within an organization is the people who comprise it. The very diversity of the experience of these people is a valuable asset, if organizations can only find a way to harness the experience and use it.

KNOWLEDGE MANAGEMENT

Another concept within the realm of learning at the organizational level that bears examination is the idea of knowledge management. Generally, people think of Knowledge Management as though it were like Information Technology and just good for storing data. Others think of Knowledge Management as more like a library and experts at collecting and organizing published information. However, in today's complex organizations there is an increasing need to manage not just data or information, but also knowledge. Knowledge is formed by people who are able to produce information from data, and then merge information and experience into knowledge (Malhorta, 2005). "Information is data put into context . . . Only when information is combined with experience and judgment does it become knowledge" (Probst, Raub, & Gibbert, 2001, p. 29). Knowledge is often undocumented. It can easily be lost if an individual who has certain knowledge is unavailable or leaves the organization.

Determining the best way to capture and manage knowledge requires collaborative partnerships.

The process of Knowledge Management (KM) takes a comprehensive, systematic approach to the information assets of an organization by identifying, capturing, collecting, organizing, indexing, storing, integrating, retrieving and sharing them (Kay, 2000). Probst, et al., (2001) further identify these organizational assets as (a) the explicit knowledge such as databases, documents, environmental knowledge, policies, procedures and organizational culture; and (b) the tacit knowledge of its employees, their expertise, and their practical work experience. The KM process strives to make the collective knowledge, information and experience of the organization available to individual employees for their use, and to inspire them to contribute their knowledge to the collective.

Knowledge management has many aspects: the conversion of the latent or tacit knowledge of its employees into articulated knowledge; the extraction of new knowledge from existing data stores through data mining; the recovery of knowledge lost in complex and diverse systems; the organization and structure of knowledge for efficient storage and retrieval; the exploitation of environmental knowledge for competitive intelligence; the coordination and integration of the content of information systems, activities and environments; and the capture of knowledge-how, procedural knowledge, in addition to knowledge-about, factual knowledge in organizations (Strassman, 1999). Therefore, KM can be a strategy that turns an organization's intellectual assets, including its recorded information, its memory, and the expertise of its employees, into greater productivity and increased competitiveness. And, while KM generally is not considered a component of organizational learning, it can be a valuable tool to help manage the process.

CONCLUSION

The world seems to be changing faster and faster—from available technologies to the increasingly global scope of interactions. The problems facing organizations as a part of a global

community seem to be growing ever more complex and seri-
ous. The challenge is how to navigate such change. Organizations—groups of people who come together to accomplish a
purpose—hold an important key to these challenges. Organizational learning can provide a way for organizations to fulfill
their function effectively, and encourage people to reach their
full potential.

With the increased intensity of global competition the pressure to produce is also intensified. Whether the product is defined as services or goods, the general tendency in the workplace is to view time spent on specific task completion as the
only legitimate form of work. Meetings are often experienced
as time "away from the real work," and therefore as time wasted.
Social interactions, whether they are informal hallway conversations, or more formal meetings specifically designed for the
purpose of reflective thinking, amplify this concern. The net
results of this can be a focus on adaptive learning rather than
generative learning.

Organizational learning requires very strong leadership as
opposed to management. At the top of the organization, this
translates into a strategic, visionary focus on the part of leaders
who are cognizant of trends in their industry, the needs of their
customer or client populations, and the context in which their
organization is functioning. Through carefully structured processes, individuals and teams are on-board with the organizational vision, and are asked to interpret it locally at the team,
department, or division levels. This shared interpretation then
provides the context within which autonomous decisions are
made and personal creativity flourishes.

Bereiter (2002), Giesecke (2004), Kirkwood and Pangarkar
(2003), and West (1994), for example, conclude that this changing paradigm in the workplace has created an environment that
emphasizes learning as the core activity of organizations. Organizational learning may be the model of the future for organizations that champion generative learning over adaptive learning.
West believes that for workers to produce knowledge, organizations will have to move toward rewarding cooperation and
collaboration rather than competition between individuals. Align-

ment, shared mental models, and constant reflection on underlying assumptions will be major foci of group learning in the workplace. Bereiter asserts that the world of work is changing and instead of learning particular jobs, employees must begin to learn about working under different conditions, in multiple roles, and on multiple teams.

Learning at the organizational level is even more critical to success in today's environment. A failure to attend to the learning of groups and individuals in the organization spells disaster in this context. Organizations need to invest not just in new machinery or technologies to make production more efficient, but in the flow of know-how that will sustain their business. Organizations need to be good at knowledge generation, appropriation and utilization.

Kansas hospital using new tech to scan prescript.

CHAPTER 6
Moving From Training to Workplace Learning

The challenges associated with the changing nature of work and the workplace environments are very real. Rapid change requires a skilled, knowledgeable workforce with employees who are adaptive, flexible, and focused on the future. One of the key responsibilities of a manager is to develop the staff of the organization. However, organizations that rely solely on training courses to meet their staff development needs are doomed to failure. In today's global market, a successful organization needs enlightened, empowered workers who have the necessary knowledge and skills to meet an ever increasingly sophisticated consumer base.

A top-down fact-dominated, mechanistic approach to learning will no longer produce what is needed in organizations. Tobin (1997) concludes that the dominance of the classroom-based training course is no longer appropriate for a global economy where change happens so quickly and with such regularity that classroom-based learning soon becomes out of date. He asserts that successful organizations are those that can persuade and encourage their people to learn how to learn—to seek actively to acquire the skills necessary to enable constant learning, and the accompanying desire to make use of these skills.

Sugrue, O'Driscoll, and Blair believe that,

Learning is a discretionary behavior. . . . You can't make someone learn just by sticking them in a classroom, no matter how fancy the presentation equipment and however slick the presenter. You can train someone to use a piece of equipment, or to adhere to a dress code. But if you want them to understand and respond to the changing needs of customers, and to help improve processes, they have to want to learn and to share learning with others. Nobody has to learn, and if you want people to do more than show up in the morning, get through the day and go home again, then you're going to have to persuade, incentivise, encourage and support them until they want to learn. Getting this message across, from the boardroom to the front line manager, and everywhere in between, is the challenge facing managers at all levels in business and government. (2005, p. 51)

The nature of learning changes because ready-made solutions to problems are fewer and less obvious in the increasing complexity of work. This places a premium on an employees' ability to work themselves out of problems. In addition, workers and organizations are finding that the line between work and learning is becoming blurred. Learning is part of work; in fact, learning is an output of work, not just an input. Activities such as on-the-job coaching, developmental assignments, sharing of lessons learned, and assigning real work to learning-project teams can be used to tap the learning potential in work situations. These informal, unstructured situations are precisely the way adults learn best. The capacity to learn continuously has become the main source of competitive advantage for many organizations. This means the most promising route for greater productivity lies in learning in better and easier ways that improves employees' abilities to solve problems, innovate, and change. Therefore, the T&D departments that are responsible for cultivating the organization's intellectual assets need to undergo a change in purpose and activities and begin to facilitate the efforts of self-directed workplace learners.

TRANSFORMATION INTO
A LEARNING DEPARTMENT

As the global workforce becomes more focused on self-directed learning and the e-learning revolution continues, (training will begin to pale in comparison to workplace learning.) Workplace conditions will force workers to learn-how-to-learn, and they will have to become skillful in the application of informal and incidental learning. In turn, these skills will help individuals become more flexible in anticipating and adapting to changes brought on by new technology, new work techniques, and rapidly changing customer preferences. The old-style training department will be forced to concentrate on helping workers acquire better skills in how they learn in the workplace. For these reasons, training departments will need to take a leadership role and champion the shift from training to workplace learning (Ashton, 2004).

As organizations attempt to cope with rapidly changing competitive conditions, managers will be looking for strategies to transform their traditional and sometimes bureaucratic, and therefore slow, organizations into institutions that have the capacity to encourage individual learning and organizational adaptation. Time has become a critical factor and speed is of the essence (Giesecke, 2004). In the future, competitiveness will rely on the ability to anticipate and rapidly adapt to dramatic shifts in customer preferences, market conditions, technology changes, and other components in the external environment (Norris, 2003).

At the same time, organizations will be forced by the dynamic external environment to focus on organizational learning. This will include finding better ways to utilize the collective knowledge of the organization (Giesecke, 2004). In fact, organizations will be clamoring for innovative ways to contribute to their effectiveness. (Even non-profits and government agencies will be vying for critical resources.) This will require new ways to meet the old as well as new challenges. Organizations will need to tap into the incredible creative abilities of their workers. One way to accomplish this task is to use the traditional vehicles of learning as well as some not-so-traditional ones. These methods will include training and education, but also other learning interventions such as coaching, mentoring, job rotation programs, online learning communities, and communities of practice (Norris, 2003). A broad approach to workplace learning can provide the means by which to explore new approaches, generate new ideas, and come up with creative solutions that will help lead the organization to new markets, new products, innovative services, and new approaches to meet client needs.

The training department, as it is now conceptualized in most large organizations, has traditionally served an important role to help workers become enculturated into a new organization, and to disseminate the accumulated wisdom of the organization's experiences. But to meet the needs of organizations in a fast-changing global economy, training departments will need to add new roles to the traditional one—the roles of learning catalyst and learning facilitator. That will transform the old-style training department into a new, invigorated learning department founded on adult learning principles that will be better equipped to promote the creative abilities of the people in the organization. This new mission will transform traditional trainers into the new role of facilitators of workplace learning whose goal will be to aid workers to achieve a rich, fulfilling work life while helping the organization to come up with creative solutions through the creation of new approaches and new knowledge.

SHIFTING FROM *TRAINER* TO *LEARNING FACILITATOR*

In moving from training to workplace learning, the first order of business will be for trainers to reflect on the role they play. They will need to see themselves totally differently than they traditionally have—a complete paradigm shift in their perspective. Instead of viewing their role as disseminator of information, they will have to start making learning happen on the job, and in real time instead of some future time. They will have to start thinking about learning as a process, rather than as a product to be delivered. This change in mind-set requires them to see their job completely differently.

To begin with, trainers will have to allow workers to accept a greater responsibility for their own learning than they traditionally have done. Once workers realize they have the freedom to initiate their own learning process to meet real-time problems and needs, they will increasingly seize the opportunity. Trainers will certainly be the ones to set the conditions to promote informal and incidental learning initiatives. To become facilitators of learning, trainers will need to become more proficient in facilitation skills rather than training skills and more proficient as enabling agents and advocates for learning. They should develop group facilitation skills as well as acquire competencies in facilitating technology-based discussions, such as videoconferencing, message boards, chat rooms, and listservs (Heron, 2005).

Trainers should challenge the idea that most learning must be planned or be organized for it to happen or for it to be useful if they are to make the transition from traditional trainers to learning facilitators. Learners will have to be taught how to become more self-directed so that they become skilled at designing their own learning objectives, developing their own resources to meet the objectives, and conducting their own evaluations so they will know when they have learned what they need to learn. Trainers will need all of their facilitation skills to show learners how to do all that. Trainers will have to build their repertoire of skills in identifying learning (rather than training) needs and finding creative ways to address the learning needs. Ashton (2004) believes that for learning facilitators to be effective in their new role, they will become especially adept at questioning learners about their learning, stimulating learners to identify their own learning needs, and helping them select the appropriate strategy to meet those needs.

Finally, trainers will draw on a large store of methods— and encourage managers and workers alike—to use them as well if they are to make the transition from trainer to learning facilitator. For example, they will not always assume that class-room-based training, e-learning, or on-the-job training will meet every learning need. They will have to become more creative and open-minded in applying a range of methods to promote learning. It will be helpful to think of all the ways that people learn on the job and in real time, be creative, and realize work-ers learn in a variety of ways. For instance, workers can learn a variety of things depending on the type of supervisor they are assigned to, the kind and variety of work they do, the kind of deadlines they are given, the types of communities of practice they are encouraged to participate in, and much more. To be a learning facilitator, trainers will need to expand their notion about workplace learning and what approaches would be ap-propriate to encourage and stimulate it.

THE PROCESS OF TRANFORMATION

Since managers and supervisors come into more frequent daily contact with workers than do trainers or workplace learn-ing practitioners, it is especially important that they function as learning facilitators as well. In fact, Gilley, Eggland, and Gilley

> believe that organizations should hold responsible for imple menting the learning process individuals who conduct em-ployee performance reviews, confront poor performance, ensure employee performance and productivity, answer for employee productivity declines, or account for organi-zational failures to meet goals and objectives. Since man-agers are accountable for these actions, they should be primarily responsible for the growth and development of employees through the application of the learning pro-cess. (2002, p. 32)

They point out that since managers are accountable for improv-ing employee performance, and are in position to provide the performance feedback and reinforcement so critical to learning transfer, they are the ones responsible for individual development (2002). Since training is often conducted away from the workplace, managers and supervisors may feel that training is someone else's responsibility. Because many learning opportunities arise in the course of work, not in the classroom, managers and supervisors need to understand the importance of taking advantage of every learning opportunity. For example, when it is time to change the settings on a machine for a new process, rather than just changing the settings her- or himself or telling the worker what to do, a supervisor may give the operators the specifications and the manual and let them work out the settings themselves. The supervisor would serve as a resource and a guide, but would not merely give them the answer, would not rush or press them for time, and would not punish or reprimand them if they got it wrong while they were figuring it out. Once the workers became comfortable with the process, the supervisor would no longer need to be involved—until a new learning opportunity arose.

There is a definitive process that workplace learning practitioners can follow to encourage others to become learning champions and apply the skills to real-time, on-the-job situations. To begin with, as with most change efforts, it is necessary to begin building a convincing case by explaining the need for change to the people in charge. Trainers can encourage managers and supervisors to become champions for learning by emphasizing the need for learning. This can be accomplished by informing and educating managers and supervisors on the philosophy of workplace learning, and by emphasizing the importance of their role in the workplace learning process. Being accustomed to thinking in terms of *training*, the notion of *workplace learning* may at first seem somewhat removed from daily workplace practice to managers and supervisors. It would be helpful to build a description of the activities of learning champions in order for them to have a detailed sense of what learning champions do and why they should do it. The role of a learning champion may not necessarily be immediately obvious to them. To prepare a role description, call together a focus-group of managers and supervisors for a brainstorming session.

The session can center on defining a learning champion as one who helps others learn in real time and on-the-job, followed by identifying the purpose and activities of a learning facilitator, and culminating in a role description that clearly identifies what a learning facilitator does in the specific organization. This process will help them understand that everyone should serve as a learning champion or will have the opportunity to serve as one.

After the role description has been prepared, it will be helpful to assess how well each manager or supervisor is presently performing at promoting workplace learning. It may be necessary to create an assessment instrument to collect their perceptions, and then the perceptions of their subordinates, peers, and immediate supervisors—as in the 360° evaluation. The instrument will help reveal the gaps for each individual manager and supervisor, and likely will help determine mutual needs among many of them. Once the needs have been determined, formal training can be used to help build the learning champion skills that are lacking. These shared needs can be met through classroom training, on-line training, CD-rom facilitation—or a combination of all of them as appropriate. It will be important to make sure that each learning champion fully understands the principles of adult learning (as discussed in Chapter 3), understands the concept of learning styles (both theirs and the workers), and have explored how learning is embedded informally and incidentally.

Of course, as with any training program, it would be a good idea to periodically follow up with the managers and supervisors to determine if they are enacting their role as learning champions. Brief, informal meetings will likely be the best means for conducting the follow-up. It would also be a good idea to periodically survey the workers to determine if they perceive the managers and supervisors as enacting their role successfully. Then, if additional action is required it can be provided in the form of individual counseling or refresher training, as appropriate.

Once managers and supervisors have mastered the art of promoting learning, workplace learning can become a common frame of reference by which to unite learning and change efforts for individuals, groups, and the organization. In fact, workplace learning may be the common component across many issues affecting individual learning, group learning, organizational learning, change, and even management (Giesecke, 2004). In the process, the importance of workplace learning as a key to competitive advantage may be reinforced. Naturally, as managers and supervisors become better learning champions it will be necessary for the workers themselves to become more self-directed and more proficient in learning-how-to-learn. Consequently, to promote the process of transformation, managers, supervisors, and other leaders can:

- Encourage curiosity—ask questions of workers about their work and work environment to stimulate interest.
- Prompt an initiating event—discover ways to stimulate individual and group thinking around common issues.
- Be a source of information—become a reliable resource and enabling person without mandating wokers action.
- Focus on critical issues—guide learners to emphasize the importance of an issue to individuals, the workgroup or team, and to the organization as a whole.
- Promote exploration—support workers, individually and in teams, to examine information they discover or other wise find, seeking to develop all sources of knowledge including formal, informal, and intuitive knowing.
- Encourage application—always promote experimentation with innovative approaches and opportunities to test-out their findings.
- Aid reflection—support workers in their efforts to reflect on their experiences and attain new perspectives from them, especially learning from mistakes or errors.
- Initiate Evaluation—assist workers to reflect on how they learn, how they might improve their learning capabilities, and how a learning situation encountered by an individual or a group of workers has informed the organization as a whole.

By following the guidelines above, managers and supervisors will be emphasizing the importance of the learning process. They will also be encouraging the workers to become more self-directed learners and to surface the informal learning already embedded in their daily work activities. Once informal learning is recognized and valued, it can be maximized. Knowledge builds upon itself. Thus, it becomes easier to learn the more a person knows. Learning is hardest in the beginning—the more they know the more they want to know. Learning becomes contagious.

SUPPORTING THE TRANFORMATION

After making the move to workplace learning, and facilitators, managers and supervisors are comfortable assuming the role as champions for learning, it will be necessary for the organization to properly support the effort. As discussed previously in Chapter 2, climate and culture conducive to learning is are musts. For this to happen, workplace learning facilitators will have to assume major leadership roles in the organization. In a leadership role they will be able to foster a climate that encourages workplace learning which will in turn encourage creativity, innovation, and performance—conditions conducive to a learning climate.

Given that the culture of every organization is different, it is very difficult to offer a step-by-step formula for developing a learning culture. A for-profit might be different from a not-for-profit, which might be different from an NGO or social services agency, and so forth. But all will likely have some conditions that discourage workplace learning. Their influence should be periodically charted and efforts concentrated on minimizing their impact on the organization. At the same time, efforts should be redoubled to support conditions that encourage workplace learning. Therefore, the goal will be to work on improving the organizational climate at the same time that work progresses to build individual learning competence. However, there are some general change strategies from the field of organization development that can work in this process (Gilley,

Eggland, & Gilley, 2002). The following guidelines offer some insights on how to build a climate that encourages workplace learning while reducing the influence of conditions that discourage that learning.

It is virtually impossible to attain any goal that can not be clearly envisioned (Griffin, Ebert & Starke, 2005). To help create a vision for the organization's workplace learning climate, managers and workers need to describe, in clear and specific terms, what the ideal learning climate should look like. This is also a good time to describe the ideal workplace learner. They will need to describe the distinctive features of a workplace climate that supports people to learn on the job so they can be more productive and feel a greater sense of accomplishment in their work. It may help to have everyone think of a time when they felt most encouraged to learn in order to solve workplace problems or challenges. Then try to recall what the organization looked like when it gave everyone the distinctive impression that it encouraged practical workplace learning. This resulting vision—in clear written form—should be positive, help create excitement and a "stir," and motivate efforts to make the vision a reality. As always, the vision statement should ensure that efforts to build a climate that encourages continuous workplace learning is aligned with the organization's strategic goals, objectives, and direction.

The workplace learning facilitators will then have a major leadership role to play while building awareness of workplace learning and the workplace learning climate. This is because many people will still think of a school or of training sessions when they think of a learning climate. They will also think of what they did while they were in school or how they behaved in training when they think of workplace learning. And, many times these recalled memories are not positive. It is important to help people understand that learning usually occurs during the course of work activities as individuals cope with real work-related issues, realize dreams, solve problems, and achieve goals.

However, it will take more than a one-shot approach to build awareness. It will be necessary to have a communication plan to build a sense that learning happens all the time and is as natural as breathing. The plan should be clear as to how workers can do better with learning, and how the organization can promote a climate and culture that encourage learning at the individual, group or team, and organizational levels. In addition to briefing sessions with all levels of employees, organization publications such as company newsletters and white papers can be used along with other awareness-building approaches.

Workplace learning facilitators will need to measure the results of what they do on an ongoing basis, provide feedback, and encourage participative planning to ensure credibility for the efforts to build a learning climate. One way to assess progress is to collect information about situations when the workplace learning climate of the organization or individual workplace learning contributed to getting bottom-line results in cost savings, enhanced revenue or sales, improved client services, or specific benefits for individuals. Unless this is done, both managers and workers likely will not take the initiative seriously. Building a learning climate may be viewed as just another failed organizational change effort. Therefore, learning facilitators will need to find ways to capture the learning that is taking place, feed those results back to the decision makers as well as the workers, and, all the while, making sure the participants are involved in the important decisions regarding the climate change (Griffin, Ebert, & Starke, 2005).

Finally, it is important to institutionalize efforts to improve the workplace learning climate to emphasize the initiative and give it visibility (Altmann, 2000). An effective way to accomplish this is to make sure that the focus on the learning climate is integrated into the other human resource functions such as, selection (especially during job interviews), orientation, formal training, performance appraisal, and recognition and reward programs. All workers at all levels of the organization can be asked periodically what they think about the organization's workplace learning climate. This will keep the issue at the forefront of the organization and emphasize the critical importance of the change initiative. Naturally, a strong learning climate cannot overcome all short-comings such as management incompetence, poor organizational design, inadequate feedback, reward, recognition and selection systems, or external environmental conditions, but it certainly can mitigate these problems.

Not only is it important to address conditions that inhibit the transition from training to learning, but it is also clear that organizations encourage workplace learning when workers perceive certain conditions to be present. Above all else, workers must feel that sufficient trust exists in the organization. They want to feel that as they learn they will not be penalized for the mistakes they make. Workers require sufficient time and space learning. Learning takes time and people need to know that learning is valued highly enough to allow them that time— along with a place to do it. Workers are also encouraged to learn when the organization supports such learning by providing adequate financial support. That support can come in the form of materials purchases, use of staff time, or release time to pursue learning opportunities.

Because workers need to know where to find the information they need, when they need it, good communication is also vital to encourage workplace learning. The old "need-to-know" has to be a thing of the past. Everyone needs-to-know whatever they feel will help them perform their job better. Nothing stifles learning more than hording information. Workers should feel that they will somehow be rewarded for learning. They want to feel that they will receive tangible payoffs for pursuing learning—that it will lead to increased opportunities for advancement or other, less tangible, rewards. Workers should be able to perceive that learning is a priority and that they are expected to be successful at it. And, they need to feel empowered. They want to be able to control their own fate and to experiment with creative approaches to difficult workplace problems. Only when they feel empowered and in control of their own learning is the workplace conducive to learning.

CONCLUSION

A focus on workplace learning extends the scope of the trainer significantly beyond designing and administering training programs. While formal training will remain an important competency, learning facilitation involves designing learning into a wide range of experiences, for individual, group, and organizational learning. The focus on learning, rather than training, reaches into every aspect of the organization from the selection process to rewards and recognition to the training classroom itself. The challenge is to build a learning climate that meets the needs of the workers while being relevant to the strategic direction of the organization. For organizations that realize their competitive advantage is their knowledge-base or that operate in a dynamic environment, the very essence of the organizational climate will have to be permeated with learning.

Exactly what it means to have a climate conducive to learning and the best way to achieve that climate will vary depending on a number of factors. Bryans and Smith (2000, p. 233) do, however, offer a few core competencies that will be common to all situations, including "1) capturing learning through knowledge-management systems and corporate practices; 2) targeting key people for development; 3) careful assessment of experience for purposes of improvement, including double-loop learning through surfacing and challenging underlying premises; 4) openness to contradictory views and opinions around important issues; and 5) focusing on data (both quantitative and qualitative) for testing attributions and assertions about events and people." Of course, there can be considerable variation in the way that these characteristics manifest themselves within a particular organization. Organizations that place a high value on individualism and competitiveness may manifest learning in ways very different from those whose competitive strategies rest on cooperative teamwork.

Regardless, moving an organization from the notion of training to one of workplace learning built into the culture and climate extends beyond the formal classroom and beyond instructional design. Rather, it reaches to the heart and soul of the organization and it penetrates the knowledge creation process in the organization. Trainers become learning facilitators and managers and supervisors become learning champions. Capturing learning in the most useful way for organizational-level learning is another dimension for weaving learning into the very fabric of the organization. More subtle challenges lie in seeking to capture the tacit knowledge of organizational members and converting it into explicit knowledge useful to new members and others; all this in addition to the traditional activities of designing and implementing more formal activities such as classroom learning, conferences, and, increasingly, e-learning. The future of workplace learning is now.

CHAPTER 7
The Future of Workplace Learning

Sustainable competitive advantage has proven elusive for companies in the twenty-first century. Although they have made enormous investments in technology, research, and state-of-the-art marketing, many of today's organizations continue to ignore the single most important factor in achieving and maintaining competitive success: people. Organizations with a highly committed workforce repeatedly outdistance their rivals in profits and returns, as well as in services provided (Rowden, 2002; Singh, 2005).

People and their learning are becoming more important because many other sources of competitive success are less powerful than they once were. Recognizing that the basis of competitive advantage has changed is essential to developing a different frame of reference for management and for organizational strategy. Traditional sources of success—product and process technology, protected or regulated markets, access to financial resources, and economies of scale—can still provide competitive leverage, but to a lesser degree now than in the past, leaving organizational climate, culture, and capabilities, derived from people and workplace learning, as comparatively more vital. If competitive success is achieved through people, then the skills of those people are critical.

During the course of a person's life, learning experiences are an important source of personal stimulation. Workplace learning represents a positive hope for people first entering the world of work as well as for individuals changing their work environments. Workers must learn to anticipate rapid change in their jobs, careers, work groups, and organizations. Farsightedness is learned. Given that, it is worthwhile to reflect on possible trends that may influence the growing importance of workplace learning.

CURRENT TRENDS AND FUTURE REALITIES

Bates (2005) reports a group of 32 university students from 20 countries representing the global NetGen (a.k.a., Internet Generation) gathered in Budapest for Microsoft's second annual Office Information Worker Board of the Future conference in July 2005. At the end of the conference, the group issued five predictions for what the workplace will look like in 10 years. The predictions were as follows:

1. Connectivity will be truly ubiquitous. People will be able to work virtually anyplace, at any time. Firms will support this flexibility, while employees will increasingly supply their own connected systems, blurring the line between work life and personal life.

2. Interfaces will be more natural. The user interface will become more natural, contextually intelligent and adaptive—just better.

3. Technology at home will be integrated and include all forms of entertainment. Technology's reach will extend to clothing and housewares, and personal finance will tie to the shopping experience. Consumer technology (and content) will pour into the workplace.

4. Learning will be driven by the individual. Increasing job movement will lead to greater self-initiated learning through on-demand, continually available forms of education, both formal and informal. The highly dynamic workplace will drive the need for lifelong learning.

5. Access to information will be smarter. Improved tools for discovering and using information will make possible a "collective intelligence," and managers will benefit by making better-informed decisions more easily. (p. 43-45)

Of course all of these predictions have profound implications for organizations but none so much so as number 4. It is becoming clear that the key to individual and organizational success is workplace learning. Of course not all learning occurs at work and not all competitive advantage can be attributed to learning—technology is a strong factor as well. In addition, at a time of rapid change and uber-global markets, it has become clear that the margin between failure and success is the ability to out-learn the competition. In order to out-learn competitors, individuals and organizations will need the ability to marshal their resources to adapt to change and anticipate the skills mandated by that change.

Having workers who are capable of performing at a high level does not happen by chance but, rather, requires meaningful effort. Individuals need to take planned or unplanned action to achieve the desired results. Learning is an important way for workers to achieve continuous improvement, from what they learn and how they learn. The current trends in the marketplace are making the role of the learner more important. It is becoming increasingly important to focus on what roles, competencies, and outputs are essential to the success of workplace learners in learning experiences rather than concentrating exclusively on the roles and competencies for trainers, HRD practitioners, or workplace learning facilitators. Simply put, trainers, and others, cannot be successful unless the learners themselves are successful, and it is incumbent upon the decision makers in the organization to ensure that the proper organizational conditions are present to guarantee that success. The role of the individual in her or his own learning is becoming more important as technology enables the available of unformation to anyone at any time, and at any place.

Therefore, in organizations today and tomorrow, workers, then, will increasingly need to take charge of their own learning rather than leave that responsibility to others. The focus of training departments will shift to showing people how to become more effective in their learning processes instead of how to master subject matter and improve performance through skill acquisition. This will have the effect of causing learning to be increasingly recognized as critical to individual and organizational success. The individual will view learning as a means to stay current in the knowledge and skills critical to their careers among an explosion of knowledge, information, and ideas. The organization will view learning as a means to harness the benefits of experience. Organizations will even look for ways to induce or stimulate situations that will allow people to anticipate change as well as react to it. The current interest in intellectual capital and knowledge management is simply the recognition that the fruits of experience and creativity are critical to present and future organizational and individual success. (Tulgan, 2002).

The new perspective will mean that workplace learning will assume a broader definition. The traditional notion that "training" and "working" are distinct entities will vanish in the future *since both will share learning in common.* As a result, workplace learning will become synonymous with any effort from which people learn deliberately through planned means (formally or informally) or accidentally through unplanned means (incidentally) as serendipitous by-products of experience. Workplace learning will be viewed then not only as traditional training efforts, but also as what people learn from those they have worked with, what customers and clients they have served, what products and services they have dealt with, in what geographical regions they have worked or what geographical based clients they have dealt with, how well they have performed their job, and why they have worked in the area in which they worked. The challenge facing organizations will be to capture this learning and channel it into useful directions, and to track who has demonstrated learning in the work-related areas.

As learning becomes more fully integrated into work, the partitions between the workplace and other spheres of life will crumble. Technology is the two-edge sword capable on knocking down communication barriers. Satellites make it possible to use a cellular phone to call a person—not just a place—anywhere on the globe, even at 100 feet below the ocean's surface or even on the moon. Wireless technology even allows people in developing countries to communicate anywhere and anytime (Evans, 2005).

There is every indication that this trend will continue. As the dream of broadcast-quality videoconferencing from every desktop becomes a reality and even more advanced technology moves from the drawing board to the marketplace, experts on virtually any subject will be available on demand. The concept of "the workplace" will no longer be associated with a physical place. The workplace is just as likely to be the sofa at home, an automobile, or in an airplane as to be behind a desk in an office, or on a production line. In many organizations work is already occurring anywhere and anytime. As a result, workplace learners will be seeking out useful information to help them perform their jobs whenever and wherever they need it. Learning is just as likely to occur during leisure activities as it is during purposeful work. Therefore, the opportunities must be available on demand.

As the walls come down between workplace learning and the other aspects of life, learners will increasingly expect real-time gratification when they recognize the importance of learning something new or experience curiosity. They will likely not have the patience to wait for formal, planned learning events. What Havighurst (1961) identified as *teachable moments*—when people are primed to learn because they face an immediate problem—will come to be recognized as *learnable moments*—when people take the initiative to act to meet their own learning needs. They will initiate steps on their own to surf the Web, network with others, or take other proactive steps to learn what they want, with whom they want, when they want, how they want, and where they want. They will also determine why they want to learn.

As instructional technology improves to keep up with this trend, things will only advance faster. Learners will have miniaturized computers built-in to their glasses or sewn into their clothing so they can access real-time coaching during the performance of their duties, and receive feedback immediately following. Organizations are already able to PodCast audio coaching to a worker's IPod—video is on the way. Learning will become recognized as an integral part of doing a job, and doing the job will be recognized as an integral part of learning. Also, group learning experiences will shift from being a time to come together to discuss what went on in the past, to opportunities to generate new ideas and new information that can lead to breakthroughs in organizational performance.

Through this mechanism, work groups and teams will become one of many approaches by which to organize and direct learning experiences. In a seminal work that has guided our understanding of learning, Houle (1961) identified the main reasons why people undertake learning projects. He discovered that some people pursue learning for social purposes while some people pursue it for the sheer love knowledge itself, and some people pursue learning to meet life-related or work-related goals. Since work and learning will become integrated and occur in real time workers will look to "social groups"—such as work groups or teams—as a natural place and context for learning experiences. Approaches as action learning will become more common (Dilworth & Willis, 2003). Action learning for example, relies on teams or groups as a context for cross-development of individual and group learning.

In seeking social groups to support their learning, individuals are seeking employers who encourage learning. Competitive wages and good working conditions will still be important, but employees will be looking for more. At a time when career resiliency will be the key to maintaining employability, workers tend to act in their own self-interest. Add that to the sense that the "psychological employment contract" between the worker and the organization may be viewed as day-to-day, it is obvious that workers will prefer employers who encourage learning that will enhance future employment prospects both inside and outside their current situation. Organizations that encourage learning in ways that contribute to workers' current performance while also enhancing their marketability will become the employer-of-choice for the most talented workers with the best ideas. For these reasons, organizations will find it

necessary as never before to promote and maintain environments that support workplace learning by providing relevant
formal learning classes, providing support like tuition reimburse-
ment, interesting work assignments, and other ways by which
the workers can develop themselves. The organizations can
make the work assignments interesting by making learning and
development objectives as important as the performance outputs so that it is obvious what is in it for the worker. On-going
emphasis on informal and the resultant incidental learning can
help accomplish this. And organizations will need to strive to
become learning organizations.

Of course, the reverse is also true—organizations will seek
out individuals who are willing to take charge of their own
learning as well. The managers will come to view learning and
development as important tools for lowering costs and improv-
ing customer satisfaction. They will increasingly seek individuals who are proactive about their learning and cultivate talents
that will benefit both the organization and the individual. The
organization will show little tolerance for workers who must be
mandated to participate in training or learning experiences. They
will, in turn, covet workers who are highly motivated on their
own to seek out and manage their own learning. The organization's
success will be tied to its ability to unleash human potential,
harness human creativity, and win the talent war for attracting
and retaining talent (Tulgan, 2002).

To stay competitive in the talent wars, organizations will
start to focus on learning ability, not educational attainment—
which are not necessarily the same. Educational attainment is
measured by the amount of formal schooling, not by openness
to learning and change, motivation to learn, or facility in the
learning process. As organizations focus on workplace learning,
the distinction will become increasingly apparent as a worker's
success will ultimately be tied to learning ability rather than less
appropriate measures such as years of schooling. The challenge
for organizations will be to find ways to measure or capture that
ability.

Of course, any measure of learning ability will need to be
culturally appropriate. Cross-cultural differences in learning style

will need to be widely explored. The same norms that influence work habits, attitudes about authority, attitudes about achievement and performance, and what constitutes appropriate awards will also influence workplace learning. For example, in much of Asia schooling and learning are viewed in the traditional sense that favors the "expert" model where the teacher is highly respected and rarely questioned. There is some movement toward a "Westernized" view that is less formal, but most still favor the traditional perspective. There is also likely to be increased attention to cross-cultural differences in learning style and especially to gender communication styles that affect learning styles, among other things. A global workforce mandates a global perspective in all matters, including learning.

Just as all learning styles will be considered instructional, technology will begin to encompass all senses and will be paired with expert systems. Up until this point instructional technology has mostly concentrated on the senses of sight and touch. Learners interact with a keyboard or touch a sensitive screen and then view a computer screen. With the recent improvement in sound cards, hearing is being added as another element. But, in an effort to engage the learner's interests and engage the multiple intelligences (Gardner, 1993) that relate to learning, all senses will be involved. In addition to enhancements to applications intended to expand the use of sight, touch, and hearing, there will be new efforts to engage the sense of taste and smell (Bates, 2005). The more sophisticated applications of virtual reality will allow workers to experience a "simulated world" that can engulf all the senses and give the learner the opportunity to "practice" before being required to perform. This is already a reality in some places such as the flight simulators that pilots use for practice. It is not even possible to speculate on all the possibilities that a wireless Web and miniaturization will bring.

Thus, changes in learning technology are coming so fast that they may be obsolete by the time they are written about. While it is true that many trends point toward the growing importance of workplace learning, none may be as profound as the changes to the workers themselves.

EXAMINING THE WORKPLACE LEARNER

Bennis (1997) has repeatedly said that leaders are only as good as their followers. If that is the case, then it can also be said that workplace learning facilitators are only as good as the learners they serve. With that statement, this discussion lends itself to the examination of who the workplace learners of tomorrow are and begs a look at what distinguishes them from other learners.

To begin at the end, learners, in the workplace or otherwise, have been referred to by a variety of terms—adult learner, distance learner, lifelong learner, self-directed learner, problem-based learner, the new learner, and so forth. Although these terms work well in specific situations, they come together well to create a new persona—the *New Era Emancipated Learner.* The New Era Emancipated Learner (NEEL) takes the initiative to learn on his or her own, and is free of, or emancipated from the constraints of the formal training mind-set. When faced with an immediate problem, these NEELs will structure their own learning experience to solve the problem. They do not need or necessarily want training or a trainer. The New Era Emancipated Learner poses a unique challenge for workplace learning facilitators as well as managers and supervisors.

New Era Emancipated Learners do not rely on planned learning experiences scheduled and organized by others. They do not necessarily rely on support or assistance from supervisors or other institutionalized providers such as workplace learning facilitators or educators. They use their own initiative to seek out the knowledge, skills, and abilities to meet their needs. They display little loyalty to any organization, team, or even a lengthy series of courses an organization may have developed. They do not stay somewhere just because it is where they started. Just as New Era Emancipated Learners take control of their careers and do not leave it up to their supervisor, they also will not just sit by and allow their learning experiences to be determined by a trainer. They take control of their own careers and learning by accessing the tremendous resources of the World Wide Web. They want the information immediately available that will help them solve problems and meet their learning needs. Of course, they face the daunting challenge of sifting through the vast amounts of data available to find the pieces that will be useful to them.

In their learning as with most other aspects of their life, they want instant gratification. They want immediate solutions to problems, personal as well as work-related. They are highly ambitious people who are driven to succeed. They are not attracted to organizationally sponsored learning experiences or educational courses that are not offered in a time or place or in a format that suits their immediate needs. They want their learning to be like satellite TV or their TIVO—on-demand that they can access whenever they want, however they want, and wherever they want.

The New Era Emancipated Learners will seek the fastest means to get a solution if they confront a problem. As long as it is not mandated, they will not sign up for a training course because it takes too long. They prefer to go to their coworkers for answers or to go to the Web. They are skilled at asking people the right question to get the information they need at the right time. They know how to use search engines and metasearch engines (where several search engines can be queried at once) to find practical information. They are searching for immediate learning on demand. They have little patience for long-term learning experiences over lengthy time spans. The learning should come in bite-sized chunks just like a sound-bite on television. They have little use for the theoretical, and gravitate to the practical when it helps them find employment or advance their careers.

Because of these tendencies, they do not take well to training. They do not like having to be officially nominated for a formal training class by their supervisor. New Era Emancipated Learners go way beyond the notion of self-directed learners who have been the focus of attention for a number of years. New Era Emancipated Learners are aggressive in their pursuit of meeting their immediate needs and are comfortable seizing the initiative to meet their own needs.

In sum, the unique characteristics that distinguish New Era

Emancipated Learners from other learners are:

- They are highly motivated to meet their own learning needs—much more so than a traditional learner. They will jump into action as soon as a problem appears. They are very self-assured concerning their learning.
- They are persistent enough to sort through mounds of useless information on the Web to find what they really want. They are very nimble at jumping from one source to another just as they jump from site to site on the Web to find something useful. They tend to learn the same way they watch television—using the remote to flip from channel to channel, all the while skimming in sound bites and watching multiple programs simultaneously.
- All of that makes them tend to want learning on demand, with learning resources and information just-in-time to help with their problems. They do not want to plow through lengthy courses, in face-to-face format or online either.

Needless to say they are comfortable using technology. They will usually start out using the Web to research a problem because of ease of accessibility, but they will eventually gain mastery of other technologies and resources—software, hardware, books, online courses—that they encounter to along the way. They possess a strong self-concept, value their own experience, and are problem driven in their approach to learning. They concentrate on learning those things for which they perceive that they can immediately use. While the tendencies of the current New Era Emancipated Learner are fairly well known, it might also be useful to explore what the future may hold for them.

WHAT THE FUTURE MAY HOLD

Without question, New Era Emancipated Learners are now, and will continue to be virtual learners. They want learning on demand and they use technology as a tool to achieve that end.

They still want to learn from and with their colleagues, but even then technology is often involved. They use Ipods, PDAs, wireless laptops, cell phones with Web access, satellite phones with Web access, and whatever is the latest technological advance. Their goal will be to find coaching or immediate answers to problems they confront. They can be patient when seeking the information they need, but are very impatient with the technology. They want better and faster Web connections and a Web that operates like television, with limitless search capabilities. They will eventually become more diverse, representing every age group, educational level, and geographical location. NEELs will be found in all professions and fields.

Three dominant trends will shape the future of NEELs: technology, demographic change, and institutional offerings. Technology will likely be the driving force in many areas. NEELs will want artificially intelligent and easy-to-use screens, easy-to-use help (immediate access to automated and human help), and blended sources of information—electronic, print, human, and so forth. The rise of the video IPOD will marry video, the Web and wireless technology to make learning truly accessible any place, at any time, and in any format.

Although it is true that younger people generally are more comfortable using technology, age will probably not be a factor in workplace learners. Today's young people have grown up with the Internet and the Web whereas their parents grew up with television. As the first "baby-boomers" reach retirement age and find that they have inadequate retirement funds, they may seek second, third, or fourth careers in telecommuting fields. Then both younger people and older people will be using the Web for real-time learning, finding jobs, and carrying them out—all on the Web. They will expect learning experiences to match this lifestyle.

To match this lifestyle, NEELs will find distance education and learning more appealing than traditional courses. One reason is that distance education—especially e-learning—can be linked to any resource, and this is not always done in traditional classrooms. The distance education programs, which Walton (1999, p. 217) defines as "a collection of innovative approaches to the delivery of instruction which are remote from their teacher," continue to experience tremendous growth. No data exists that details the exact number of such programs, but estimates place accredited distance programs of all types at between 90 million and as high as 700 million (Sugrue, O'Driscoll, & Blair, 2005). Estimates also place the number of participants at around 100 million who are engaged in some form of planned distance learning program (Slotte, Tynjala, & Hytonen, 2004). Norris (2003) reports that several studies found these programs to be working quite well. Of course, NEELs will not limit their learning to formal distance education as they also tend to be excellent at networking with other people as a learning source as well.

Along with this greater understanding of workplace learners, it is easy to expect that they will continue to want their learning experiences to be short, to the point, practical, and on demand. While they require access to high tech solutions, they also will want high touch. They will become more skilled at finding ways to structure information for easier access and more contact between individuals and groups. The ultimate goal is online interactivity.

This will require workplace learning facilitators to make their offerings stand out from others. Learning opportunities will have to be built around problems and solutions, or problem-oriented questions and solution-oriented answers, rather than linear sequences with little practical application. Many of the same approaches that work for e-customers will likely work for NEELs. Organizations will need to utilize expert systems that document how more experienced workers have solved problems, and Electronic Performance Support Systems (EPSS), which puts everything they need at their fingertips (Gery, 2001), are especially appealing as tools for workplace learning. This means that workplace learning facilitators will have to be keenly aware of the needs and desires of NEELs and will have to cater to them.

Clearly, there is a growing importance on focusing on the workplace learning process and the workplace learner. Workplace learners are taking their own initiative to seek out learning opportunities without relying on support or assistance from their immediate supervisor, and without relying on formal learning experiences organized and scheduled by the organization. This makes it clear that focusing on training is not enough. Now, and in the future, the workplace learner will have to be the crux of attention if organizations are to survive and thrive.

CONCLUSION

Now more than ever, competitive advantage comes from the ability to transform ideas into value—through process innovation, strategic insights, and customized services. The nations of the world are evolving toward a diverse yet unified global market, with customers, partners, and suppliers who work together across cultures and continents. The global workforce is always on and always connected—requiring new tools to help people organize and prioritize their work and personal lives. Transactions are becoming more transparent, with a greater need to ensure accountability, security, and privacy within and across organizations. And a generation of young people who grew up with the Internet is entering the workforce, bringing along workstyles and technologies that feel as natural to them as pen and paper to earlier generations. All of these changes are giving people new and better ways to work, but they also bring a new set of challenges: a deluge of information, constant demands on their attention, new skills to master, and pressure to be ever more productive (Evans, 2005).

These trends underscore the dominant theme underlying all organizational issues now and in the future: the primacy of the individual as learner. According to a report from the Center for Workforce Development (1998), workplace learning

> is interpreted as an approach to learning, training, and upgrading based on the individual's ability to sense what is relevant and important, and use them: to be flexible in viewing things, and independent in thinking, curious, initiating, and persistent. (p. 103)

Individual responsibility for workplace learning is further extended in the need for workers to manage their own careers. Each worker is expected to take the initiative in obtaining additional knowledge so that he or she can contribute to the ongoing development of the organization as well as improve his or her own job prospects (Bates, 2005).

Despite the apparent increased interest in workplace learning, it has existed for quite some time, in one form or the other. Over the years, the form and type of learning have changed, as have the labels used to describe it. The current wave of workplace learning incorporates many aspects of learning not previously considered. Of particular interest is the emphasis given to the issues of learning to learn and learning as a group.

In order for workplace learning to take place, organizations have to modify their climate so as to encourage workers to operate in a learning mode. This is true for any organization—whether it is for-profit, non-profit, government agency, social service agency, or others—for all are essentially the same even if their purpose is different. Organizations need to design ways to encourage workers to test out assumptions that arise from their daily work experiences, an important aspect of the ongoing process of learning (Marsick & Watkins, 1993). Tobin's (1997) concept of the "knowledge-enabled organization" places workplace learning at the very heart of the organization when he says,

> when a company learns to utilize and foster the growth of the knowledge and skills of all employees across all functions and levels, integrate learning activities into every employee's work, encourage and reinforce all modes of learning, and align all of this learning with the company's strategic business direction, it becomes a knowledge-enabled organization. (p. 30)

Senge (1990) attaches an almost mythical quality to the ability of workplace learning to fundamentally transform people and the places where they work. Blackler and McDonald extend the concept by asserting, "A learning organization is a place where, through learning, people are continually re-perceiving their world and their relationship to it, discovering how they create their reality and their future" (2000, p. 103). Underlying organizational learning, like workplace learning, is the belief in continuous learning for continuous improvement. A learning organization emerges as a result of the intentional action of the organization in its attempts to transform itself through a variety of learning. All learning is directed toward some desired result, involves the encouragement of thinking and group learning, and is a transformative process. To take organizational learning to its ultimate conclusion is to develop a community of learners, or community of practice.

Learning in organizations is also about leadership and preparing for the realities of the fast-advancing future. In the face of shrinking workforces, many organizations are finding they need to do more with less. Any organization that is not using or at least exploring the use of blogs, wikis, folksonomies, social network systems, RSS aggregators, and podcasts is missing out on wonderful open-source applications on the Internet. A blog post is a learning object. Davenport (2006) notes that,

> In part because of the nature of today's organizations and in part because of individual preferences, informal learning has become more important. As a consequence, the range of interventions undertaken by the trainer now extends far beyond the design and delivery of the training course. There has been a huge increase in coaching and in ways of promoting group learning. (p. 41)

A world that no longer exists is certainly one way to describe the HRD or workplace learning field of yesterday compared to where it will be a few years from now.

Individuals are increasingly shouldering responsibility for their own learning as a result of the dynamic changes in the workplace, changing employer-employee relationships, and more widely available on-demand learning opportunities produced through mind boggling advances in instructional technologies. The growing numbers of New Era Emancipated Learners are posing new challenges to organizational trainers. They go way beyond the concept of the self-directed learner as they pursue their own development. They are more likely to want on-demand learning than to look to educational providers they have used in the past. They want to meet their learning needs the moment they recognize them.

The future belongs to the workplace learners who willingly assume responsibility for their own learning. The trainer who has served as intermediary in the past between the learner and the subject area has been removed from the learning equation. Therefore, trainers must become more masterful at facilitating on an individual basis. Trainers are faced with a changing workplace as NEELs become the norm rather than the exception.

These emerging trends have forever banished the days when "trainers" can be viewed as the corporate "school teachers." If workplace learners are to take more control of their learning, those responsible for workplace learning must increasingly become facilitators and helpers to encourage the process. Workplace learning facilitators will assist line managers, teams or work groups, and individuals to conduct their own needs assessment, construct their own learning objectives, determine their own desired outcomes, select or develop their own instructional resources, and evaluate their results so that they can determine when they are finished. This will allow the workplace learning facilitators to function more as change agents and enabling agents to help others meet their own needs in real time. Therefore, the success of the workplace learning facilitator will not be measured by how many "trainees" they place in classroom seats (seat-time), but their success will be viewed as a function of how successful workers are in creating and maintaining cutting-edge skills and finding creative solutions to solve real-time work problems. So, just as in life—one person dies and another is born to take her or his place—so too it happens in the workplace. The days of the corporate trainer have passed and the days of the workplace learning facilitator are upon us.

REFERENCES

Altmann, R. (2000). Forecasting your organizational culture. *Journal of Property Management, 65*(4), 60–65.

Argyris, C. (1991). Teaching smart people how to learn. *Harvard Business Review, 69*(3), 99–109.

Argyris, C. & Schon, D. (1978). *Organizational learning: A theory of action.* New York: Harper-Collins.

Argyris, C. & Schon, D. (1996). *Organizational learning II: Theory method & practice.* Reading, MA: Addison-Wesley.

Arnold, J., Cooper, C. & Robertson, I. (1995). *Work psychology: Understanding human behavior in the workplace.* London: Pitman.

Ashton, D. (2004). The impact of organizational structure and practices on learning in the workplace. *International Journal of Training and Development, 8*(1), 43–53.

Bass, B. (1990). *Bass and Stogdill's handbook of leadership.* New York: Free Press.

Bates, S. (2005, July). Managing talent—future forum: Emerging trends. *HR Magazine,* p. 42–49.

Bell, C. (1977). Informal learning in organizations. *Personnel Journal, 56*(6), 280–283.

Bennis, W. (1997). *Organizing genius: The secrets of creative collaboration.* Reading, MA: Addison-Wesley.

Bereiter, C. (2002). *Education and mind in the knowledge gap.* London: Lawrence Erlbaum.

Billett, S. (2002). Critiquing workplace learning discourses: Participation and continuity at work. *Studies in the Education of Adults, 34*(1), 56–67.

Billington, D. (1998). *Ego development and adult education.* Doctoral Dissertation, The Fielding Institute. Dissertation Abstracts International, 49(7). (University Microfilm No. 98-16, 275.

Blackler, F. & McDonald, S. (2000). Power, mastery, and organizational learning. *Journal of Management Studies, 37*(6), 833–851.

Blenkin, G. & Kelly, A. (1981). *The primary curriculum.* London: Harper and Row.

Boud, D. & Garrick, J. (1999). *Understanding learning at work.* London: Routledge.

Boud, D., Solomon, N., Leontios, M. & Staron, M. (2001). Tale of two institutions: Exploring collaboration in research partnerships. *Studies in the Education of Adults, 33*(2), 135–142.

Brookfield, S. (1986). *Understanding and facilitating adult learning.* San Francisco: Jossey-Bass

Bryans, P. & Smith, R. (2000). Beyond training: Reconceptualizing learning at work. *Journal of Workplace Learning, 12*(6), 228–235.

Candy, P. (1991). *Self-direction for lifelong learning.* San Francisco: Jossey-Bass.

Castka, P., Bamber, C., & Sharpe, J. (2003). Measuring teamwork culture: The use of a modified model. *Journal of Management Development, 22*(1/2), 149.

Center for Workforce Development (1998). *The teaching firm: Where productive work and learning converge.* Newton, MA: Education Development Center.

Clemmons-Rumizen, M. (2002). *The complete idiot's guide to knowledge management.* Madison, WI: CWL Publishing Enterprises.

Conlon, T. (2004). A review of informal learning literature, theory and implications for practice in developing global professional competence. *Journal of European Industrial Training, 28*(2/3/4), 283–295.

Courtney, S. (1989). Defining adult and continuing education. In S. Merriam & P. Cunningham (Eds.). *Handbook of Adult and Continuing Education* (pp. 15–25). San Francisco: Jossey-Bass.

Cseh, M., Watkins, K., & Marsick, V. (1999). Reconceptualizing Marsick and Watkins' model of informal and incidental learning in the workplace. In P. Kuchinke (Ed.). *Proceedings of the Annual Conference of Human Resource Development* (pp. 348–351). Baton Rouge, LA.

Davenport, R. (2006). Future of the profession. *Training & Development, 60*(1), 40–45.

DeSimone, R., Werner, J., & Harris, D. (2002). *Human Resource Development* (3rd Ed.). Mason, OH: South-Western.

DiBella, A. & Nevis, E. (1998). *How organizations learn: An integrated strategy for building learning capabilities.* San Francisco: Jossey–Bass.

Dilworth, R. & Willis, V. (2003). *Action learning: Images and pathways.* Malabar, FL: Krieger.

Dodgson, M. (1993). Organizational learning: A review of some literatures. *Organization Studies, 14*(3), 375–394.

Dumphy, D., Turner, D. & Crawford, M. (1997). Organizational learning as the creation of corporate competencies. *Journal of Management Development, 16*(4), 232–245.

Easterby-Smith, M. & Araujo, L. (1999). *Organizational learning II: Theory, methods, and practice.* Reading, MA: Addison Wesley.

Easterby-Smith, M., Snell, R., & Gehardi, S. (1998). Organizational learning: Diverging communities of practice. *Management Learning, 29*(1), 5–20.

Ellinger, A. (2004). The concept of self-directed learning and its implications for human resource development. In B. Yang (Ed.). *Contributions of adult learning theory to human resource development* (pp. 159-177). Advances in Developing Human Resources, 6(2), Sage.

Evans, J. (2005). Jobs and globalization: Promise or threat. *The OECD Observer, 249*, pp. 23.

Fenwick, T. (2001). Tides of change: New themes and questions in workplace learning . *New Directions for Adult and Continuing Education, 92*(1), 3–17.

Fisher, T. (1995). Self-directedness in adult vocational education students: Its role in learning and implications for instruction. *Journal of Vocational and Technical Education, 12*(1), 1–12.

French, W. & Bell, H. (1995). *Organization development: Behavioral science interventions for organizational improvement* (5th Ed.). Englewood Cliffs, NJ: Prentice Hall.

Fulmer, R., Gibbs, P., & Keys, B. (1998). The second generation learning organization: New tools for sustaining competitive advantage. *Organizational Dynamics, 27*(2), 6–21.

Gardner, H. (1993). *Multiple intelligences: The theory in practice.* New York: Basic Books.

Garrick, J. (1999). *Informal learning in the workplace.* London: Routledge.

Garrison, D. (1997). Self-directed learning: Toward a comprehensive model. *Adult Education Quarterly, 48*(1), 18–34.

Garvin, D. (1994). Building a learning organization. *Business Credit, 96*(1), 19–28.

Gephart, M., Marsick, V., Van Buren, M., & Spiro, M. (1996). Learning organizations come alive *Training and Development, 50*(12), 35–45.

Gery, G. (2001). *Electronic Performance Support Systems: How and why to remake the workplace through the strategic application of technology.* Boston: Weingarten.

Giesecke, J. (2004). Transitioning to the learning organization. *Library Trends, 53*(1), 54–67.

Gilley, J., Eggland, S., & Gilley, A. (2002). *Principles of human resource development* (2nd Ed.). New York: Basic Books.

Grantham, C. & Nichols, L. (2003). *The digital workplace: Designing groupware platforms.* New York: Van Nostrand Reinhold.

Griffin, S., Ebert, G., & Starke, E. (2005). *Business* (5th Ed.). New York: Prentice Hall.

Hackman, J. (1990). *Groups that work (and those that don't).* San Francisco: Jossey-Bass.

Havighurst, R. (1961). *Developmental tasks and education.* New York: David McKay Publishing

Hedberg, B. (1991). *How organizations learn and unlearn.* New York: Oxford University Press.

Heron, J. (2005). *The facilitator's handbook.* New York: Kogan Page.

Houle, C. (1961). *The inquiring mind*. Madison: University of Wisconsin Press.

Industry Report. 2003. *Training, 39*(10), 37–82.

James, L., James, I., & Ashe, D. (1990). The meaning of organizations: The role of cognition and values. In B. Schneider (Ed.), *Organization climate and culture* (pp. 40–84). San Francisco: Josey-Bass.

Jarvis, P. (1987). *Adult learning in social context*. Beckenham, UK: Croom Helm.

Jones, J. (1981). The organizational universe. In J. Jones &W. Pfeiffer (Eds.). *The 1981 Annual: Developing Human Resources*, (pp. 155–164). San Diego, CA: University Associates.

Kaplan, R. & Norton, D. (1996). Strategic planning and the balanced scorecard. *Strategy and Leadership, 24*(5), 18–24.

Karahanna, E., Evaristo, R., & Srite, M. (2005). Levels of culture and individual behavior. *Journal of Global Information Management, 13*(2), 12–32.

Kasl, E., Marsick, V., & Dechant, K. (1997). Teams as learners: A research-based model of team learning. *Journal of Applied Behavioral Science, 33*(2), 227–246.

Kay, A. (2000). By any other name. *Knowledge Management, 3*(7), p.8.

Kirkwood, T. & Pangarkar, A. (2003, May). Workplace learning—beyond the classroom. *CMA Management*, pp. 10–12.

Knowles, M. (1970). *The modern practice of adult education: Andragogy vs. pedagogy*. New York: Cambridge Books.

Knowles, M. (1975). *Self-directed learning*. New York: Association Press.

Knowles, M. (1980). *The modern practice of adult education: From pedagogy to andragogy* (2nd Ed.). New York: Cambridge Books.

Knowles, M. (1984). *The adult learner: A neglected species* (3rd Ed.). Houston, TX: Gulf Publishing.

Knowles, M. (1989). *The making of an adult educator*. San Francisco: Jossey-Bass.

Knowles, M., Holton, E., & Swanson, R. (1998). *The adult learner: The definitive classic in adult education and human resource development*. Houston, TX: Gulf Publishing.

Lakoff, G. & Johnson, M. (1980). *Metaphors we live by*. Chicago: University of Chicago Press.

Lave, J. & Wenger, E. (1991). *Situated learning: Legitimate peripheral participation*. Cambridge, UK: Cambridge University Press.

Leslie, B., Aring, M., & Brand, B. (1998). Informal learning: The new frontier of employee and organizational development. *Economic Development Review, 15*(4), 12–18.

Lesser, S. & Storck, L. (2001). Communities of practice and organizational performance. *IBM Systems Journal, 40*(4), 831–841.

Lien, M. (2003). Workforce diversity: Opportunities in the melting pot. *Occupational Outlook Quarterly, 48*(2), 28–38.

Malhorta, Y. (2005). Integrating knowledge management technologies in organizational business processes: Getting real time enterprises to deliver real time business performance. *Journal of Knowledge Management, 9*(1), 7–28.

Marques, J. (2005). Socializing a capitalistic world: Redefining the bottom line. *Journal of American Academy of Business, Cambridge, 7*(1), 283–288.

Marsick, V. & Watkins, K. (1990). *Informal and incidental learning in the workplace*. London: Routledge.

Marsick, V. & Watkins, K. (1993). The learning organization: An integrative vision of HRD. *Human Resource Development Quarterly, 5*(4), 353–360.

Marsick, V. & Watkins, K. (1997). Lessons from incidental and informal learning. In J. Burgoyne & M. Reynolds (Eds.). *Management learning: Integrating perspectives in theory and practice* (pp. 228–243). Thousand Oaks, CA: Sage.

Marsick, V. & Volpe, M. (1999). The nature and need for informal learning. In V.

Marsick & M. Volpe (Eds.), *Informal learning on the job* (pp. 1–9). San Francisco: Berret-Koehler.

McLagan, P. (1989). Models for HRD practice. *Training and Development Journal*, 41–53.

Merriam, S. & Cafarella, R. (1999) *Learning in adulthood* (2nd Ed.). San Francisco: Jossey-Bass.

Mezirow, J. (1985). A critical theory of self-directed learning. In S. Brookfield (Ed.). *Self-directed learning: From theory to practice* (pp. 17–30). New Directions for Continuing Education, No. 25. San Francisco: Jossey-Bass.

Nador, S. (2001, October 22). The fine art of team selection and development. *HR Reporter*, pp. 2–3.

Norris, S. (2003) *Workplace learning: An assessment of approaches to learning and perceptions of the learning environment in two public health organizations.* Unpublished doctoral dissertation. Queen's University at Kingston (Canada).

Nystrom, H. (1990). Organizational innovation. In M. West & J. Farr (Eds.). *Innovation and creativity at work* (pp. 143–161). New York: Wiley.

Pedler, M., Burgoyne, J., & Boydell, T. (1991). *The learning company: A strategy for sustainable development.* London: McGraw-Hill.

Peled, A. (2000). Politicking for success: The missing skill. *The Leadership and Organization Development Journal, 21*(1), 20–29.

Peters, T. & Waterman, R. (1984). *In search of excellence: Lessons from America's best-run companies.* New York: Warner Books.

Pfeffer, J. (1998). *The human equation: Building profits by putting people first.* Boston: Harvard Business School Press.

Porter, M. (1990). *The competitive advantage of nations.* New York: Free Press.

Prahalad, C. & Hamel, G. (1990). The core competencies of the corporation. *Harvard Business Review, 68*(3), 79–91.

Prange, C. (1999). Organizational learning: Desperately seeking theory. In M. Easterby-Smith & J. Burgoyne (Eds.). *Organizational Learning and the Learning Organization* (pp. 21–36). London: Sage.

Probst, G., Raub, S., & Gibbert, M. (2001). *Managing knowledge.* London: Sage.

Raelin, J. (2000). *Work-based learning: The new frontier of management development.* Englewood Cliffs, NJ: Prentice Hall.

Robbins, H. & Finley, M. (1995). *Transcompetition: Moving beyond competition and collaboration.* New York: McGraw-Hill.

Rowden, R. (1995). The role of human resource development in successful small to mid-sized manufacturing businesses: A comparative case study. *Human Resource Development Quarterly, 6*(4), 355–373.

Rowden, R. (2000). The relationship between charismatic leadership behaviors and organizational commitment. *The Leadership and Organization Development Journal, 21*(1), 30–35.

Rowden, R. (2001). The learning organization and strategic change. *SAM—Advanced Management Journal, 66*(3), 11–18, 24.

Rowden, R. (2002). The relationship between workplace learning and job satisfaction in small to mid-sized U.S. businesses. *Human Resource Development Quarterly, 13*(4), 407–425.

Rowden, R. & Ahmed, S. (2000). The relationship between workplace learning and job satisfaction in small to mid-sized businesses in Malaysia. *Human Resource Development International, 3*(3), 307–322.

Rowden, R. & Conine, C. (2004). The relationship between workplace learning and job satisfaction in U.S. small commercial banks. *Journal of Business and Entrepreneurship, 16*(2), 69–90.

Rusaw, A. (1995). Learning by association: Professional associations as learning agents. *Human Resource Development Quarterly, 6*(2), 215–226.

Salomon, G. (1993). No distribution without individual's cognition: A dynamic interactional view. In G. Salmon (Ed.). *Distributed cognitions—Psychological and Educational Considerations* (pp. 111–138). Cambridge, UK: Cambridge University Press.

Sambrook, S. & Stewart, J. (2000). Factors influencing learning in learning oriented organizations. *Journal of European Industrial Training, 24*(2/3/4), 209–219.

Schein, E. (2003). *Organizational culture and leadership* (3rd Ed.). San Francisco: Jossey-Bass

Schon, D. (1973). *Beyond the stable state: Public and private learning in a changing society.* Harmondsworth, UK: Penguin Publishing.

Schon, D. (1983). *The reflective practitioner: How professionals think in action.* New York: Basic Books.

Schwandt, D. & Marquardt, M. (2000). *Organizational learning: From world-class theories to global best practices.* Boca Raton, FL: St Lucie Press.

Seely-Brown, J. & Duguid, P. (2001). *Organizational learning and communities-of-practice: Toward a unified view of working, learning and innovation.* New York: Institute of Management Sciences.

Senge, P. (1990). *The fifth discipline: The art and practice of the learning organization.* London: Random House.

Senge, P. (1996). Leading learning organizations. *Training and Development, 50*(12), 46–54.

Singh, S. (2005). Globalization puts focus on HR. *Canadian HR Reporter, 18*(11), 1–2.

Slotte, V. Tynjala, P., & Hytonen, T. (2004). How do HRD practitioners describe learning at work. *Human Resource Development International, 7*(4), 481–499.

Solomon, N., Boud, D., Leontois, M., & Staron, M. (2001). Re searchers are learners too: Collaboration in research on workplace learning. *Journal of Workplace Learning, 13*(7), 274–281.

Sorohan, E. (1993). We do, therefore we learn. *Training and Development, 4*(10), 47–52

Stamps, D. (1998). Learning ecologies. *Training, 35*(1), 32–38.

Stata, R. (1999). Organizational learning: The key to management innovation. *Sloan Management review, 40*(2), 71–86.

Storck, J. & Hill, P. (2000). Knowledge diffusion through 'strategic communities.' *Sloan Management Review, 41*(2), 63–74.

Strassman, P. (1999). What's the worth of an employee? *Knowledge Management, 2*(12), p. 14.

Sugrue, B., O'Driscoll, T., & Blair, D. (2005). What in the world is WPL? *Training and Development, 59*(1), 51–52.

Taylor, B. (1995). Self-directed learning: Revisiting an idea most appropriate for middle-school students. In *Proceedings of Combined Meeting of the Great Lakes and Southeast International Reading Association* (pp.395–407). Nashville, TN.

Tennant, M. (1999). *Psychology and adult learning* (2nd Ed.). London: Routledge.

Tobin, D. (1997). *The knowledge-enabled organization.* New York: American Management Association.

Toll, D. (1999). *Workplace learning: An assessment of approaches, perceptions, and outcomes.* Unpublished doctoral dissertation. Queen's University at Kingston (Canada).

Tough, A. (1971). *The adult's learning project.* Toronto: Ontario Institute for Studies in Education.

Tulgan, B. (2002). *Winning the talent wars.* New York: W. W. Norton.

Von Krogh, G., Ichijo, K., & Nonaka, I. (2000). *Enabling knowledge creation: How to unlock the mystery of tacit knowledge and release the power of innovation.* Boston: HBS Press.

Walton, J. (1999). *Strategic human resource development.* Essex, UK: Pearson Education Limited.

Watkins, K. & Marsick, V. (1992). Toward a theory of informal and incidental learning in organizations. *International Journal of Lifelong Education, 11*(4), 287–300.

Watkins, K. & Marsick, V. (1993). *In action: Creating the learning organization.* Alexandria, VA: American Society for Training & Development.

Wellins, E. (1991). *Empowered teams: Creating self-directed work groups that improve quality, productivity, and participation.* San Francisco: Jossey-Bass.

Wenger, E. (1991). Communities of practice: Where learning happens. *Benchmark, 3*(3), 6–8.

Wenger, E. (1998). *Communities of practice: Learning, meaning and identity.* Cambridge, UK: Cambridge University Press.

Wenger, E. (2002). *Cultivating communities of practice.* Cambridge, MA: Harvard University Press.

West, G. (1996). Group learning in the workplace. In S. Imel (Ed.), *Learning in groups: exploring fundamental principles, new uses, and emerging opportunities* (pp. 15–29). New Directions for Adult and Continuing Education, No. 70. San Francisco: Jossey-Bass.

West, P. (1994). The concept of the learning organization. *Journal of European Industrial Training, 18*(1), 15–20.

Wolfe, P. & Brandt, R. (1998). What do we know from brain research? *Educational Leadership, 56*(3), 8–13.

Yukl, G. (1994). *Leadership in organizations* (2nd Ed.). Englewood Cliffs, NJ: Prentice-Hall.

INDEX

Action Learning, 118
adult learners, 44
Altmann, R., 22, 23, 108
andragogy, 42, 44
    assumptions of, 42–44
    comparison to pedagogy, 45
Argyris, C., 87
Argyris, C. & Schon, D., 32, 79, 80,
    81, 82, 89
Arnold, J., Cooper, C. &
    Robertson, I., 2
Ashton, D., 82, 99, 101

Bass, B., 24, 25, 120
Bates, S., 114, 127
Bell, C., 51
Bennis, W., 19, 23, 59, 85, 121
Bereiter, C., 13, 94, 95
Billett, S., 2, 3, 13, 19, 39
Billington, D., 33
Blackler, F. & McDonald, S., 23,
    127
Blenkin, G. & Kelly, A., 15
blog, 128
Boud, D. & Garrick, J., 39, 40, 65
Boud, D., Solomon, N., Leontios,
    M. & Staron, M., 70
Brookfield, S., 44, 46
Bryans, P. & Smith, R., 3, 40, 59,
    110

Business Process Outsourcing
    (BPO), 28

Candy, P., 46
Career Development (CD), 9
Castka, P., Bamber, C., & Sharp, J.,
    27, 28
Center for Workforce Develop-
    ment, 51, 126
Clemmons-Rumizen, M., 71, 72
collaborative learning, 58–60, 76,
    83
communities of practice, 66–75
    assumptions, 70
    defined, 66
    dimensions of, 68
    fostering, 72
Conlon, T., 39, 40
Cseh, M., Watkins, K., &
    Marsick, V., 50, 51, 52

Davenport, R., 128
DeSimone, R., Werner, J., &
    Harris, D., 4, 57, 77
DiBella, A. & Nevis, E., 77
Dilworth, R. & Willis, V., 118
Dumphy, D., Turner, D. &
    Crawford, M., 1

Easterby-Smith, M. & Araujo, L.,
    80–81, 88

Easterby-Smith, M., Snell, R., &
    Gehardi, S., 1, 59
Electronic Performance Support
    Systems (EPSS), 125
Ellinger, A., 46
environmental factors, 19–31
    external, 26–31
        globalization, 27–29
        outsourcing of jobs, 28
        sociocultural forces, 30
    internal, 20–25
        climate, 22
        culture, 21
        leadership, 24
        structure, 23
    learning climate—and
        developing, 31–36
Evans, J., 28, 29, 117, 126

Fenwick, T., 6, 39, 59
Fisher, T., 48, 49, 53
formal learning, 7
French, W. & Bell, H., 61
Fulmer, R., Gibbs, P., & Keys, B., 1,
    19

Gardner, H., 120
Garrick, J., 13, 19
Garrison, D., 52, 53
Garvin, D., 86
Gephart, M., Marsick, V., Van
    Buren, M., & Spiro, M., 86,
    87, 88, 91
Gery, G., 125
Giesecke, J., 77, 94, 99, 105
Gilley, J., Eggland, S., &
    Gilley, A., 102, 106–107
Grantham, C. & Nichols, L., 90
Griffin, S., Ebert, G., & Starke, E.,
    26, 107, 108
group (team) learning, 10

Hackman, J., 75
Havighurst, R., 117
Heron, J., 101
Houle, C., 118
Human Resource Development
    (HRD), 4, 8, 9, 10, 11–13
    defined, 5

incidental learning, 7, 49
informal learning, 7, 49–52, 56
instructional system design,
    (ISD), 11
Ipod, 118, 124

James, L., James, I., & Ashe, D., 23,
    24
Jarvis, P., 60
Jones, J., 21

Kaplan, R. & Norton, D., 87
Karahanna, E., Evaristp, R., &
    Srite, M., 30
Kasl, E., Marsick, V., & Dechant, K,
    63.
Kay, A., 93
Kirkwood, T. & Pangarkar, A., 1, 5,
    6, 94
knowledge management, 92–93
Knowles, M., 42, 44, 45, 46, 50
Knowles, M., Holton, E., &
    Swanson, R., 44, 46–47
KSA (knowledge, skills, and
    abilities), 4, 10

Lakoff, G. & Johnson, M., 11
Lave, J. & Wenger, E., 60, 66, 68,
    69, 70, 82
learning champion, 103–104
learning climate, 31, 36, 44
learning, definition of, 2
learning facilitator, 100–102

learning organization, 83–92
  five disciplines of, 84–85
learning—process, 11–17
learning—product, 11-17
legitimate peripheral participation,
  69
Leslie, B., Aring, M., & Brand, B., 2
Lesser, S. & Storck, L., 67
Lien, M., 30

Malhorta, Y., 92
Marques, J., 27, 30
Marsick, V. & Volpe, M., 4, 7
Marsick, V. & Watkins, K., 6, 7, 36,
  50, 51, 127
McLagan, P., 8
mental models, 85
Merriam, S. & Cafarella, R., 41, 44,
  60
Mezirow, J., 46
Microsoft, 114

Nador, S., 63
New Era Emancipated Learner
  (NEEL), 121–125, 128, 129
Norris, S., 2, 6, 31, 39, 63, 75, 99,
  100, 125
Nystrom, H., 34–35

organizational learning, 77–92, 128
  deuteron, 81
  double-loop, 81
  single-loop, 81
Organization Development (OD),
  4, 9

pedagogy, 41, 43, 44
  comparison to andragogy, 45
Pedler, M., Burgoyne, J., &
  Boydell, T., 83
Peled, A., 24
performance improvement, 13

personal mastery, 84
Peters, T. & Waterman, R., 25
podcast, 118
Porter, M., 25
practitioner, WpL, 10
Prahalad, C. & Hamel, G., 1
Prange, C., 91
Probst, G., Raub, S., & Gibbert, M.,
  92, 93
process—learning, 11–17
product—learning, 11–17

Raelin, J., 40, 47, 59, 86
Robbins, H. & Finley, M., 60
Rowden, R., 2, 7, 24, 78, 113
Rowden, R. & Ahmed, S., 2
Rowden, R. & Conine, C., 2
Rusaw, A., 50, 51, 75

Salomon, G., 93–94
Sambrook, S. & Stewart, J., 35
Schein, E., 1, 21
Schon, D., 60, 79, 82
Schwandt, D. & Marquardt, M., 96
Seely-Brown, J. & Duguid, P., 59,
  73
self-directed learning, 45–49, 56
Senge, P., 61, 62, 65, 82, 83, 84,
  85, 86, 87, 127
shared vision, 85
Singh, S., 28, 29, 113
Slotte, V., Tynjala, P., &
  Hytonen, T., 125
Sorohan, E., 51
Specht, L. & Sandlin, P., 46
Stamps, D., 50
Stata, R., 90
Storck, J. & Hill, P., 75
Strassman, P., 93
Sugrue, B., O'Driscoll, T., &
  Blair, D., 97, 125
systems thinking, 84

Taylor, B., 52
team (group) learning, 10, 60–65,
    76, 85
Tennant, M., 40
TiVo, 122
Tobin, D., 97, 127
Toll, D., 4, 23, 39
Tough, A., 46
Training & Development (T&D),
    4, 8, 9, 11–13, 41
training, 99, 103
    definition of, 2, 4
Tulgan, B., 25, 116, 119
2003 Training Industry Report, 2

virtual reality, 120
Von Krogh, G., Ichijo, K., &
    Nonaka, I., 19

Walton, J., 5, 124
Watkins, K. & Marsick, V., 37, 40,
    50, 77, 83
Wellins, E., 19, 23
Wenger, E., 60, 66, 68, 69, 72, 73,
    74, 82
West, G., 62
West, P., 21, 26, 86, 88, 94
Wolfe, P. & Brandt, R., 32–33
workplace learner, 121–126
Workplace Learning (WpL), 4, 8, 9,
    10, 12–13, 44, 103, 113–120,
    126, 128
Workplace Learning, defined, 6, 99
World Wide Web (www), 121

Yukl, G., 24, 25